D0014354

Unfounded Loyalty

Wayne Perryman

Unfounded Loyalty

An In-Depth Look Into the Love Affair Between Blacks and Democrats

A Fact-Finding Investigation from 1832 to 2004 covering:

The Democrats' Racist Past
The Republicans' Quest for Equality
The Power of Christianity on the African American Culture

Wayne Perryman

HARA
PUBLISHING GROUP

Hara Publishing

P.O. Box 19732
Seattle, WA 98109

Copyright ©2003 by Wayne Perryman - All rights reserved
Copyright ©2004 2nd Edition

No part of this publication may be reproduced or transmitted in any form or by any means electronic or mechanical, including photocopy, recording, or any information storage and retrieval system now known or to be invented, without permission in writing from the author, except by a reviewer who wishes to quote brief passages, in connection with a review written for inclusion in a magazine, newspaper, broadcast, or website.

Library of Congress Cataloging-in-Publication Data
Perryman, Wayne.
    Unfounded Loyalty: Questioning the Blind Love Affair Between Blacks and Democrates/Wayne Perryman.
    p. cm.
    Includes bibliography references ind index.
    "A fact-finding investigation from 1832 to 2002 covering: Democrats' racist past, the Republicans quest for equality, the power of Christianity on the African American culture."
    LCCN 2002116824
    ISBN: 1-887542-18-3
    1. African Americans--Politics and government.
    2. Democratic Party (U.S.)--History. 3. United States--Politics and government.
    I. Title
E185.P44 2003   973'.0496073
              QBI3-200145

Printed in the United States
10 9 8 7 6 5 4 3

Contents

Using the words from the *Negro National Anthem* as the primary theme, this chapter emphasizes the relationship between African Americans and their historical reliance on God. Most African American historical figures were Christians and Republicans. The African American Culture evolved out of a Christian foundation, with faith in God and strong family values.

Integration and assimilation severely damaged the African American Culture. We became a different people. Dr. King would not know us today. We sold out our rich heritage and values for political loyalty and social acceptance, which has resulted in a multitude of social problems.

This chapter examines how government programs of the sixties affected African Americans and our community. It looks at how we trusted in government more than God to solve our problems and explores our nonadherence to our historical beliefs and teachings. This chapter also weighs the pros and cons of government programs and the track record of the church.

Chapter Four shows how the older generation of blacks viewed the Democratic Party that supported slavery and segregation. It delves into racist and terrorist practices by the Democrats from 1860 to 1960. This chapter discusses Lincoln's personal feelings about blacks and describes how the Radical Republicans put pressure on Lincoln to do the right thing. It reviews how the Democrats' laws and racist practices along with their connection with the Ku Klux Klan resulted in beatings, lynchings, and two landmark court cases.

This chapter considers what is happening in the Democratic Party and takes a look at Clinton and his black appointees and what his administration had done for blacks. Dr. King was not a diehard Democrat, and he strongly criticized the Kennedy administration on Civil Rights.

Blacks criticize the Congressional Black Caucus and current black leadership. Debate is entered regarding the need for new black leadership. Black leaders ignore slavery in Africa by Muslims. Dr. King is shown as a spiritual, not a political leader. Congressman Floyd Flake is the personification of a good leader. The performance of black leaders is evaluated.

Chapter Seven

Did the Democrats really fall in love with blacks after 200 years of racist practices? Democrats never apologized for those racist practices. Do white Democrats support reparation pay? Republicans who fought for the Emancipation Proclamation and equality for blacks and started programs to assist blacks are identified.

This is a historical review of faith-based programs, including the Abolitionist Movement. It features blacks and whites who made a difference, including those Whites who were the founding fathers of the NAACP, as well as those who started many of our black schools and colleges (most of whom were Republican supporters).

Chapter Nine   **Doing Things for Ourselves**   **125**
This chapter challenges African Americans to stop depending on
political parties to do what we can do for ourselves. It asks every
black professional athlete, entertainer, and politician to return to
their community once a year and participate in community projects.

Chapter Ten   **Walking by the Same Rule**   **131**
This chapter offers solutions to the problems that are now facing
African Americans, using the basic principles that worked for us in
the past.

About The Author

We selected Reverend Wayne Perryman for this project because of his track record in community service and his tremendous expertise in historical research and fact-finding investigations. Over the years, Rev. Perryman has received a multitude of awards and commendations for his research and his service to his community. His programs and services include Operation Destitution to feed the poor, Role Models Unlimited to stop gang violence, and other special projects for inner-city youth. His research includes books covering the history of the Black Race from Bible times to our present time and his fact-finding investigations have resulted in large settlements in various types of discrimination cases.

In 1989 Rev. Perryman brought together gang leaders from two rival gangs along with Washington State's most powerful black leaders and politicians to negotiate a truce. That meeting led to the formation of Role Models Unlimited and a role model recruiting banquet that attracted over 2,000 black men from all walks of life. Banquet attendees included Grammy Award winners and a number of African American professional athletes from the NBA, NFL, and Major League Baseball. Several major news organizations covered the black tie event, including *Sports Illustrated* magazine. Other major cities across the country inquired and expressed an interest in the program.

In 1993, Rev. Perryman challenged major Christian publishers with his research book entitled *The 1993 Trial on the Curse of Ham*. In his book, he proved that the publishers were wrong when they stated that, according to the Bible, *the Black Race was cursed.* The curse theory was used to justify slavery, establish Jim Crow Laws, and promote racial discrimination. Perryman's book forced two major Christian publishers and the *Encyclopedia Britannica* to remove this false theology from their publications—a theory that had existed for over three hundred years. His book, *Thought Provoking Bible Studies of the 90s,* highlighted the significant role that blacks played in Bible history, and his character-building children's storybooks (featuring Ken Griffrey Jr. and ESPN host Harold Reynolds) were the first children's storybooks to be placed in the National Baseball Hall of Fame Library.

As an employment relations consultant, he has helped a number of persons who were victims of employment discrimination but could not afford an attorney. In 1995, Rev. Perryman took on a case involving over one hundred powerful shipping companies in the Pacific Northwest. After his extensive fact-finding investigation, the cases were finally settled and his clients walked away with over four million dollars.

Perryman's past and present organization affiliations include the following:

1. Founder of Operation Destitution
2. Founder of Inner City Vision Ministries
3. Founder of Role Models Unlimited
4. Co-founder of Youth Challenge
5. Chairman of Occupational Steering Committee for Seattle Public Schools
6. Member of the National Council on Crime and Delinquency
7. United Way Loaned Executive
8. Advisory Board Member of Seattle Community College
9. Executive Director of the Regional Educational Alliance on Gang Activities for 500 schools with a population of over 300,000 students in Washington State

10. National Program Director for *Brothers,* a new program that works with African American inmates.
11. A basketball, baseball, and football coach for thirty years.
12. A Member of the Seattle Coalition, a group of pastors who sponsor projects to build and remodel homes for low income inner city single parents.

As a community activist, Rev. Perryman has received commendations from the President and Vice President of the United States, the U.S. Congress, the United States Senate, former Washington State governor Booth Gardner, and former Seattle mayor Charles Royer. In addition to this recognition, Perryman's work with children, professional athletes, gang members, and major corporations has resulted in local, national and international media coverage, including *Sports Illustrated, Parade Magazine, Sports Illustrated for Kids, The Seattle Times, Seattle Post Intelligencer, Ebony Magazine, Upscale Magazine, EM Magazine, Christianity Today, The Personnel Administrator, ABC Home Show, TBN, The 700 Club,* and *Italy's Speak Up Magazine.*

Rev. Perryman is a former recording artist, a former radio talk show host, the author of several books and publications, the father of four, Associate Minister of Mt. Calvary Christian Center Church of God in Christ, and the owner of Consultants Confidential Inc., an employment relations consulting firm.

Foreword

Perryman makes a great contribution in shedding the light on many aspects of history that are not commonly known. Covering a span of history from 1832 to 2002, Perryman's fact-finding investigation provides facts and insights that are seldom ever discussed among those seeking the black vote. Quoting from our nation's top historians, both black and white, he reveals shocking truths. Readers will learn that:

1. From 1863 to 1972, Republicans passed more Civil Rights Legislation than the Democrats and were directly responsible for the passage of the 1964 Civil Rights Act and for providing strength to Affirmative Action programs.
2. The Ku Klux Klan was the terrorist arm of the Democratic Party.
3. During Reconstruction, in an effort to discourage blacks from voting Republican, thousands of blacks were shot, beaten, hung, mutilated, and burned to death by terrorists from the Democratic Party.
4. *Plessy vs Ferguson* and *Brown vs the Board* of Education were two landmark civil rights cases that were designed to overturn the racist practices that were established by the powerful Southern Democrats.
5. Even though Lincoln felt that those who profited from slavery should pay for their wrong, white Democrats today say very little in support of reparation pay.

6. After President Franklin D. Roosevelt received the black vote, he banned black newspapers from the military shortly after taking office because he was convinced the newspapers were communist.

7. President Clinton sent troops to Europe to protect the citizens of Bosnia while allowing an estimated 800,000 black Rwandans to be massacred in Africa.

In addition to these powerful revelations, Perryman provides insights on:

- The powerful role that Christianity played in the African American culture
- The difference between integration and assimilation.
- The pros and cons of government programming
- How blacks were the benefactors of faith-based programs
- Perhaps most important, the contributions that the Republican Party has made to advance the cause of civil rights for African Americans.

Perryman points out that it is commonly believed that the Democrats were the ones who championed the cause of civil rights for African Americans. This myth can be traced back to the 1960s when Presidents Kennedy and Johnson threw the full weight of the federal government behind the civil rights movement, thus producing two major pieces of civil rights legislation: the 1964 Civil Rights Act and the 1965 Voting Rights Act. However what was not commonly known was that only 61% of the Democrats in the House voted for the 1964 Civil Rights Act as opposed to 80% of the Republicans. In the Senate only 69% of the Democrats voted for the Act in contrast to 82% of the Republicans. President Johnson commended the Republicans for their efforts to get his bill passed, even though powerful members of his own Democratic Party had fought against the bill.

It is true that the 1964 Civil Rights Act and the Voting Act of 1965 provided a framework for significant changes in the American civil rights policy. There were two major aspects of these laws: the adoption of the law and the implementation of the law. Among these, policy implementation has the broadest expression in advancing the cause of civil rights. From this perspective, it appears that the Democrats have been the champions of civil rights for African Americans. Perryman's fact-finding investigation dispels this deception and reports how Dr. Martin Luther King Jr. criticized President Kennedy for ignoring civil rights issues shortly after he took office.

As a professor of political science and Afro-Ethnic Studies, I have discovered that various ethnic groups in America have not been able to advance themselves from a socio-economic standpoint until the federal government stepped in and adopted positive laws to protect their freedom. This allowed many of them to connect themselves to the mainstream of society's income redistribution system, i.e., trade, commerce, and real estate. From this perspective, the Republicans have obtained more pluses than the Democrats in advancing the status of African Americans. This is one of the major points that Perryman makes in this book.

Without being connected to the mainstream, the government can adopt public policies and allocate billions of dollars to improve the conditions of African Americans. But if these measures are not directed toward capital development, and if they are not complemented with what Booker T. Washington referred to as *"Christian Character,"* they will do very little to improve their conditions. Between the two major parties, the Republican programs have provided more sustenance than those of the Democrats in protecting African Americans' freedom to connect themselves to the mainstream.

The policies adopted under the Nixon administration along with his passage of the 1972 Equal Employment Opportunity Act (which established Affirmative Action Programs) brought more African Americans into the mainstream than during any other period except the Reconstruction. What the Affirmative Action Program did was to grant African Americans the freedom to interact in an entrepreneurial environment. In doing so, they were able to acquire the necessary managerial skills to operate a successful business.

Unfortunately, the Republicans' record on civil rights was tarnished by selective reports on history, by Watergate, and later, by the anti-civil rights advocates that flocked to the Republican camp during the Reagan administration. Whenever they noted racial progress, the new anti-civil rights advocates sought to reverse it and encouraged the Republican Party to adopt a policy of racial exclusion. Many of these individuals remained in these positions until Republicans decided to abandon their unwritten racial exclusion policy during President George H. W. Bush's administration.

I feel the Republican Party stands to gain greater political dividends if they were to expand their policies of inclusion. This will help to diffuse bloc voting for Democratic candidates by African Americans. Inclusion policies directed toward African Americans (particularly those associated with the black church) will go a long way to advance the Republicans' goals in solving social problems, such as reducing welfare, crime, and socially dependent programs. Republicans must understand that despite African Americans' disenchantment with the mistreatment of the Democratic Party, a carrot-and-stick approach will not work.

African Americans are becoming more politically mature and economically independent than they have been in the past. Consequently, the practice of treating them with disrespect and contempt will no longer work. To lure them among their ranks, both parties must seriously consider becoming more moderate and adopting a policy of racial inclusion. Such a policy would significantly promote the public good.

Perryman's book, more than any other, provides a framework and a vehicle for both political parties to rethink their civil rights policies toward African Americans. But more important, it is an eye opener to those who have compromised their cultural Christian values for party loyalty.

To every reader, I say as King Solomon said in Proverbs 3:3: *"Let not mercy and truth forsake thee: bind them about your neck; write them upon the table of thine heart"* (KJV).

J. Owens Smith, Ph.D.
California State University, Fullerton, CA

Acknowledgements

I owe my deepest gratitude to all those (both Democrats and Republicans) who provided invaluable information during this fact-finding investigation, and to others who provided critical reviews, editing services, and support in a variety of other ways to make this project a success. To the following people I want to say *thank you* from bottom of my heart.

Professor Leroy Johnson of Northwest College
Professor and Mrs. Phillip Dunston of University of Washington
Dr. and Mrs. Brown of Iowa State University
Dr. Cecelia Harris
Ed Decker
Hal and Elizabeth Hansen
Rev. Aaron Haskins
Mr. and Mrs. Morrison
Mark Phelps, attorney at law
Hattie Greensburg
Miss DeVitta Dorsey
Miss Kori D. Chandler
Miss Shannon Smith
Mrs. Heidi Lewis
Rev. Charlie Young
Miss Cheri "Pavi" Dawson

Special thanks to Professor James McPherson of Princeton University for allowing me to use much of his work.

Introduction

Of the few books that I have had the privilege to author or co-author, this writing assignment was by far the most difficult one. It was not something that I wanted to do. I had just finished a book that had taken me three years to write. I was tired and couldn't fathom the thought of doing another research book so soon. A close friend of mine from the D.C. area, who is also a registered Democrat, insisted that I do this project. He wanted me to address the spiritual, political, cultural, and economic issues affecting African Americans.

My record will show that I am neither Democrat nor Republican, nor am I for or against many of our most powerful black leaders. I try to stand on neutral ground and evaluate each person and each situation on its own merits. In the past I have been a speaker at conferences where Republican Congressman J.C. Watts and Ambassador Alan Keyes were featured guests, and in contrast I have delivered endorsement speeches for local Democratic candidates who were my classmates. I voted for President Clinton and served on the Committee of Washington State's Black Clergy To Re-elect Clinton. For most of my adult life, I have voted Democrat and never known the true history of the Democratic Party until I completed this fact-finding investigation.

The aim of this publication is neither to condemn nor endorse any political party. My purpose is to remind us of some historical truths that we tend to overlook and to enlighten us regarding current matters that are often ignored by biased media. I am certainly not one who is without fault or one who is in a position to cast stones at others. The Bible tells us *"there is not a just man on earth that doeth good and sinneth not"* (Ecclesiastes 7:20). We all have faults and everyone makes mistakes. My only goal is to provide truth, not condemnation.

The Bible also says, *"the truth shall set us free"* (John 8:32) if we know the truth. I'm confident that if the truth is told, freedom will be the result. We will be free to make the right political choices; free to acknowledge and honor those individuals who laid down their lives for us; free to embrace our faith in God and the black church that represents God's love; free to love and appreciate one another as true brothers and sisters. But most of all, we will be free to face the truth, accept the truth, and deal openly with the truth.

The truth will tell us that in 1968, Democratic Governor George C. Wallace received no support from black voters when he entered the race to become the President of the United States. Blacks felt they could not support an unrepentant man who was openly opposed to blacks having the same rights as whites. The truth will tell us that during the past forty years, blacks have given their support to a party that has never repented of promoting, supporting, and financing a holocaust that sent millions of blacks to the grave. The holocaust was slavery—the party was Democrat.

In his book, *Black Americans*, historian John Hope Franklin says: *"It has been estimated that 900,000 slaves were imported in the 16th century, 2.75 million in the 17th century, seven million in the 18th century, and four million in the 19th. Whatever the estimates, the total number of Africans removed from their native land ran into the millions. When one considers the many recruits who must have been killed while resisting capture and the vast numbers who died during the Middle Passage, together with the millions who were successfully brought to the Americas, the aggregate approaches a staggering figure. Whether the figure is 15 million or 50 million, it is a grim testimonial to the fabulous profits that were realized, the ruthlessness with which the trader operated, and the great demand for slaves."*[1] Abolitionist Thomas Clarkson claimed, that the average loss of life during the shipment of slaves was 12.5 percent. He reports that during one shipment of 7,904 slaves, 2,053 died before reaching America. These figures suggest that millions of blacks died enroute to America.

In 1854, the issue of slavery inspired the formation of the Republican Party. The party had two top priorities: (1) to stop the advancement of the slave trade into the new Northern states, and (2) to completely abolish it, if possible. While the Republicans fought to abolish it, the Democrats fought to maintain it. During slavery, in addition to working from sunup to sundown, our wives, mothers, and daughters were raped and otherwise sexually abused, while our sons, fathers, and husbands were beaten and hanged. They were treated so badly that, in some cases, the plantation's animals received better care than the slave. While Christian abolitionists, along with Republicans (often the two were one and the same), joined forces to **ban it** (slavery), the Democrats invested millions of dollars and gave their lives to **expand it**.

When the Civil War ended, angry Democrats continued their efforts to disenfranchise African Americans, while many Radical Republicans moved down South to protect them. Professor Allen Trelease, History Professor of the University of North Carolina and author of *Reconstruction: The Great Experience,* said: *"The Democrats were everywhere the party of **White supremacy**. Most Southern whites never lost their outrage at the idea of Negro equality in general and the Negro voting and holding office in particular."*[2]

Professor John Hope Franklin of Brooklyn College said the personal indignities inflicted upon whites who supported Negroes, as well as the Negro himself, *"...were so varied and so numerous as to defy classification or enumeration. There were the public whippings, the maiming, the mutilations, and other almost inconceivable forms of intimidation."*[3]

Because the treatment of African Americans in the South was so deplorable, several Black ministers came together and wrote a letter to the citizens of the United States. The letter became part of the *Congressional Record* during the 50th Congress on August 25, 1888. The following is a portion of that letter:

"To the People of the United States:

We, citizens of New Orleans, as well as of neighboring parishes, from which we have been driven away without warrant or law, assembled in mass meeting at New Orleans, La, on Wednesday, August 22, 1888, at Geddes Hall, declare and assert: That a reign of terror exists in many parts of the state; that the laws are suspended and the officers of the government, from the governor down, afford no protection to the lives and property of the people against armed bodies of whites, who shed innocent blood and commit deeds of savagery unsurpassed in the dark ages of mankind.

For the past twelve years we have been most effectively disfranchised and robbed of our political rights. While denied the privilege in many places of voting for the party and candidates of our choice, acts of violence have been committed to compel us to vote against the dictates of our conscience for the Democratic Party, and the Republican ballots cast by us have been counted for the Democratic candidates. The press, the pulpit, the commercial organizations, and executive authority of the State have given both open and silent approval of all these crimes. In addition to these methods, there seems to be a deep scheme to reduce the Negroes of the State to a condition of abject serfdom and peonage.

These acts are done in deliberate defiance of the Constitution and the laws of the United States, which are so thoroughly nullified that the Negroes who bore arms in defense of the Union have no protection or shelter from them within the borders of Louisiana. During the past twelve months our people have suffered from the lawless regulators as never before and since the carnival of bloodshed conducted by the Democratic Party in 1868.

A single volume would scarcely afford sufficient space to enumerate the outrage our people have suffered and are daily suffering at the hand of their oppressors. They are flagrantly deprived of every right guaranteed them by the Constitution; in many parts of the State they are free only in name; they cannot assemble in places to indicate and discuss an equitable rate of wages for their labor; they do not feel safe as property holders and tax-payers, and are permitted to enjoy but very few public conveniences.

To our people we advise calmness and a strict regard for law and order. If your homes are invaded expect no mercy, for none will be shown, and if doomed to die, then die defending your life and home to the best of your ability. If convinced that you will not be permitted to live where you are in peace and perfect security, quietly go away.

Invoking the guiding favor of Almighty God and the sympathy of mankind, we are your brethren in affliction and the common bond of humanity.[4]

The letter was signed by Rev. Ernest Lyon, Rev. A.E.P. Albert, Rev. J.H. Coker, M.D., Rev. T.B. Stamps, Rev. M.C.B. Mason, Rev. W. Paul Green, Rev. J.D. Kennedy and the Rev. C.B. Wilson. The problems were so severe that President Grant had to send troops to the South to protect black voters from the Democrats and their Klan supporters.

While the Rockefeller-type Republicans and abolitionists spent millions to finance schools and colleges for the newly freed slaves, Democrats (and their Klan supporters) spent their time and energies keeping blacks out of the schools. Their tactics included murdering and beating teachers and making blacks work long hours in the field as sharecroppers. W.E.B. Du Bois said, *"had it not been for the Negro School and college the Negro would for all intent and purposes have been driven back to slavery.*"[5]   Many blacks would be surprised to learn that:

1. A number of the black schools and colleges were actually started by and named after white Republicans and abolitionists.

2. The first black elected officials after the Civil War were Republicans, not Democrats.

3. The founding fathers of the NAACP were themselves white, and were individuals who supported the Republicans' efforts to assist African Americans.

As of this date, few leaders have acknowledged the unselfish and unpopular contributions that both the Republicans and the Christian abolitionists made on behalf of African Americans. Nor have they acknowledged the fact that no formal apology has ever been offered by the Democratic Party for their role in oppressing and killing African Americans both before and after the Civil War. Governor George Wallace was forgiven, because he eventually acknowledged his wrong and asked for forgiveness. The Democratic Party should feel obligated to do the same before asking for the black vote. Failure to do so would be the same as a Ku Klux Klan candidate asking for the black vote without ever denouncing his past racist practices and without ever acknowledging the damage that he had done to the African American people. Technically speaking, at one point in history, the Klan and the Democrats were one of the same, with just different names.

The Native Americans received compensation and land rights for the injustices they suffered. The Japanese Americans received reparation pay for the injustices they suffered. The United States Government worked to recover money owed to the Jews resulting from their Holocaust. But no one has held the Democrats accountable for the holocaust that took the lives of millions of African Americans. Nor has anyone ever asked the Democrats to compensate

African Americans for the injustices and the pain that they were forced to endure.

This is not to say that **all** Democrats are or were evil, and **all** Republicans are or were good. The facts are provided only to cite the truth. In this publication I examine the following:

1. The Democratic and Republican track records for addressing the needs of African Americans
2. The problems that were caused by integration
3. Our history of having faith in God and not Government
4. Lincoln's image of blacks and his vacillation on the issue of slavery
5. The declining impact and membership of the black church
6. The history of faith-based programs
7. Black leaders who turned their backs on black longshore workers
8. President Clinton's refusal to comply with a court order that required that his Secretary of Labor force Northwest shipping companies to develop an Affirmative Action Plan
9. Questions regarding the effectiveness of Black Leadership
10. The accountability report card to evaluate all leaders and organizations
11. Dr. King's low marks on President Kennedy's Civil Rights achievements
12. What we must do to turn things around

My goal is to inform, not to indict. It is to provide truth, not perpetuate lies. It is to provide hope, not despair. It is not to say that one party is better than another, nor is it my intention to endorse either the Democratic or Republican Party. It is to help African Americans understand that it was our faith in God, not our faith in government or a political party that made our families strong, our communities peaceful, and our children respectful. Our faith in God inspired us, strengthened us, and enabled us to overcome seemingly insurmountable odds to excel in every area of endeavor. Our faith inspired us, sustained us, unified us, guided us, and provided us with a sense of security. It was the foundation on which a great culture and a great people were built and it was, and always will be, the secret to our success.

Chapter One

Our Demise Was Prophesied

In Seattle, an African American minister stood in the wings off stage waiting for his introduction as the keynote speaker at an inner city high school during the celebration of Black History Month. Just before he went on stage, the vice principal standing next to him whispered, *"Remember, it is against school policy to talk about religion in a public school."*

The minister turned to her and said, *"The next time you ask a person to come to your school to speak on Black History, I want you to remember this: It is easier to remove the blackness from our skin than it is to remove God from our history." (See Appendix G 1787-1802)*

The minister's response was based on historical fact and the inspiring words from James Weldon Johnson's famous poem, *Lift Every Voice and Sing*. This poem, which recognizes the relationship between our God and our history, became what is now known as the "Negro National Anthem." In the third verse of his poem, Johnson highlights the role that God has played in the lives of African Americans. Johnson writes:

God of our weary years,
God of our silent tears.
Thou who hast brought us thus far on the way,
Thou who hast by Thy might
Led us into the light,
Keep us forever in the path, we pray.

1

Lest our feet stray from the places,
our God, where we met Thee,
Lest our hearts, drunk with the wine of the world,
we forget Thee.
Shadowed beneath Thy hand,
May we forever stand,
True to our God,
True to our native land.

Like a prophet with a pen, Johnson warns black Americans never to stray from the God "*who hast brought us thus far.*" Many have ignored his warning, while others were never taught that there is a direct correlation between our history and our faith in God. Hosea the prophet says, "*Our people are destroyed because of the lack of knowledge.*" And because they lack knowledge about their history and their God, they will "*reject the God*" (Hosea 4:6) that brought their ancestors through difficult times. Such seems to be the case with today's African Americans.

Far too many blacks do not understand the significance of James Weldon Johnson's poem or the role that our faith in God has played in the development of our people. According to Psychology Professor Nancy Boyd Franklin, our spiritual roots did not begin in America, they began in Africa. In her book, *Black Families in Therapy,* she writes, "*Because religion was such an integral part of man's existence* [in Africa]*, it and he were inseparable. Many African languages did not have a separate word for religion. Religion accompanied the individual from conception to long after his physical death.*"[6] Both Franklin and Johnson believe African Americans have always relied on their spiritual beliefs to get them through hard times. While Franklin believes our spiritual roots can be traced back to Africa, other scholars traced them back to the Garden of Eden, believing that Adam and Eve were black. Because we were spiritual people long before our feet touched American soil, it was not difficult to transfer our African spiritual orientation to believing in a greater and more powerful God.

James Weldon Johnson
This poet wrote *Lift Every Voice and Sing,* also called the
"Negro National Anthem."

The Christian Faith and Historical Figures

Our faith in God has always been the inspiring factor that empowered so many of our people to do great things.   When it came to dealing with problems, many of our famous black historical figures depended on the providence of God rather than on the promises of government. This is not to say that African Americans merely went to church and prayed and did nothing but wait for *manna* to fall from heaven. During and after slavery, we were taught from the Holy Scriptures, *"Faith without works is dead"* (James 2:20). So we prayed while we built secret compartments in wagons and secret rooms in homes, and dug underground tunnels as part of the Underground Railroad. We prayed while we mapped out routes for our escape. We prayed while some distracted the overseer just long enough so that others could disappear into the nearby forest in their quest for freedom. Even as we ran, we continued to pray.

Blacks included prayer as a part of everything they did. Even poet James Weldon Johnson included the following prayer in his poem:

"Keep us forever in the path, we pray.
Lest our feet stray from the places, our God,
where we met Thee,
Lest our hearts, drunk with the wine of the world,
we forget Thee.
Shadowed beneath Thy hand,
May we forever stand,
True to our God,
True to our native land."

In addition to prayer, blacks were taught from Scripture, *"If in all their ways they acknowledge God, He would direct their path"* (Proverbs 3:6). In their quest for freedom, many of our great historical figures applied the Scripture and did *"acknowledge God,"* and many have testified that God directed their path. The following are just a few of those who acknowledged God.

Booker T. Washington

Booker T. Washington's mother acknowledged God every night during her prayer time. Booker reported that, night after night, he would hear his mother praying for freedom and for the day her son would be able to go to school and get an education. Her prayers were soon answered.

From the age of nine to fourteen, Booker worked mornings from 4 AM to 9 AM in a coal mine, then went to a nearby one-room school. After school, he returned to the mine to finish his long shift. In 1872, when he was accepted into Hampton Normal Agricultural Institute, he walked and hitchhiked some five hundred miles just to enroll. Shortly after he graduated from Hampton, a church gave him the job as principal of their school. The school was later called the Tuskegee Institute, the home of another God-fearing African American named George Washington Carver.[7]

George Washington Carver

Like Booker T. and his mother, Carver also complemented his prayer life with hard work. When the sun set on his life, this praying man left a multitude of products that changed the face of America, Carver is also credited with saving the beautiful cherry trees along Pennsylvania Avenue in front of the White House. In the book, *George Washington Carver - An American Biography*, author Rackham Holt tells of Carver's religious upbringing as a child:

> *"Sometimes she* [Aunt Moriah] *took little George to the African American Methodist Church, which she attended. The preacher, whose name was Givens, could not read a word and had to have someone else read the text for him, but he was a*

good man. He actually lived what he preached and made a profound impression on young George. Aunt Moriah could read perhaps a little, but she prayed a great deal and instilled in her foster son [George] her devotion to the Word of God. When he was nearly eighty years old, he was still reading the Bible she gave him, keeping the place with the bookmark he embroidered under her vigilant eye."[8]

The author recalls a time when young George took his accordion to a friend's house and how they sang gospel songs into the evening. He said, *"George joined the family worship, and the father of the home prayed for George's health and his happiness in the Christian faith."* In a letter to some very close friends, Dr. Carver wrote the following: *"I am taking better care of myself than I have. I realize God has work for me to do, so consequently, I must be careful with my health."* As always he ended his letters with *"Your humble servant in God."*

Dr. Carver was right; God did have something for him to do, as evidenced when this man of prayer was asked to speak at the Peanut Association in Montgomery, Alabama, in September of 1920. After entering the building through the back entrance, the *"colored"* entrance, Carver gave an amazing presentation, displaying an array of products ranging from milk to leather stains, wood stains, Worchestershire sauce, cream and punch—each made from peanuts.[4] By the time his life had ended on January 5, 1943, this brilliant scholar, musician, singer, painter, and scientist had developed over three hundred products from peanuts and one hundred products from sweet potatoes. He also had traveled around the world helping other countries with their agricultural and botanical problems.

Carver attributed his success to hard work and his faith in God. He said, *"The secret to my success is found in the Bible: 'In all thy ways acknowledge Him and He shall direct thy path.' No books ever go into my laboratory. The thing I am to do and the way of doing it are revealed to me. I never have to grope for methods. The method is revealed to me the moment I am inspired to create*

Dr. George Washington Carver
He found wisdom and inspiration from God and the Bible.

something new. Without God to draw aside the curtain, I would be helpless."[9]

During Carver's visit to Washington, D.C., in 1921, a senator asked: *"Does the Bible tell about peanuts?"* And Carver replied, *"No sir, but it tells me about the God who made the peanut. I asked Him to show me what to do with the peanut and He did."*[10] When asked why he chose not to capitalize on all of his patents and discoveries by selling them, he said, *"God gave them to me. How can I sell them to someone else for profit?"* Shortly before he died, he donated his entire life savings to his foundation.

Sojourner Truth

The African American Hall of Fame of Faith honors a multitude of well-known historical figures. Around 1797 or 1799, James and Elizabeth Domefree gave birth to a little girl in Ulster County, New York, and named her Isabella.

As a child, Isabella was abused by several of her masters. As a young woman, Isabella said she saw visions and heard the voice of God. At the age of twenty-seven, Isabella had a dramatic conversion to Christianity and attended John Street Methodist Church and the Black African Methodist Episcopal Zion Church in New York City. As a woman of God, she traveled throughout the North speaking against slavery and exhorting her listening audience to accept the biblical message of God's goodness and the brotherhood of man. Isabella was her birth name, but Sojourner Truth was her name of fame.[11]

Harriet Tubman

Another individual enshrined in the Hall of Fame of Faith is a woman christened by her parents as Harriet, but whom historians called *"Moses."* Harriet Tubman was born in Dorchester County,

New York, in 1820. She was a devout Christian who trusted in God for her strength and guidance to help her lead over three hundred slaves to their freedom. Her mission to free her people was initiated by her own escape to freedom at the age of twenty-nine. She was a woman who not only led her people, she also encouraged them to press on and to never give up.[12]

During a speech, Tubman said, *"I always told God I'm going to hold steady on to You and You got to see me through. Just so long as He wants to use me, He'll take care of me. And when He don't want me any longer, I'm ready to go."*[13]

Frederick Douglass

On September 22, 1848, the *Liberator* published a letter from one of the most powerful abolitionists in America, Frederick Douglass. The following is a portion of the letter that he wrote to his former slave master.

"When I was six years old, I saw the slave driver whip a slave woman, cut the blood out of her neck, and heard her piteous cries. I went away into the corner of the fence and wept and pondered over the mystery. I had, through some medium, I know not what, got some idea of God, the Creator of all mankind, the black and the white, and that He made the blacks to serve the whites as slaves. How could He do this and be good, I could not tell. I was not satisfied with this theory, which made God responsible for slavery, for it pained me greatly, and I have wept over it long and often. Your wickedness and cruelty committed in this respect on your fellow-creature are greater than all the stripes you have laid upon my back, or theirs. It is an outrage upon the soul, a war upon the immortal spirit, and one for which you must give account at the bar of our common Father and Creator. Your mind must have become darkened, your heart hardened, your conscience seared and petrified, or you would have long since

thrown off the accursed load and sought relief at the hands of a sin-forgiving God. I shall make use of you as a means of exposing the character of the American church and clergy and as a means to bringing this guilty nation with yourself to repentance. In doing this I entertain no malice toward you personally. There is no roof under which you would be more safe than mine and there is nothing in my house which you might need for your comfort, which I would not readily grant. Indeed, I should esteem it a privilege to set you an example as to how mankind ought to treat each other. I am your fellow man, but not your slave."[14]

During one speech, Douglass said: "*I loved all mankind, slaveholder not excepted though I abhorred slavery more than ever. I saw the world in a new light. I gathered scattered pages of the Bible from the filthy street gutters and washed and dried them, that in moments of leisure I might get a word or two of wisdom from them.*"[15]

Nat Turner

Nat Turner was known for the slave revolts that broke out on August 21, 1831, in South Hampton County, Virginia. But few knew of his religious convictions. Just before he was executed, he said these words: "*In 1825, I sought more than ever to obtain true holiness before the great day of judgement should appear and I began to receive the true knowledge of faith. And from the first steps of righteousness until the last…the Holy Ghost was with me.*" [16]

Benjamin Banneker

In 1791, mechanical inventor and mathematician Benjamin Banneker wrote a letter to Thomas Jefferson throughout which he made several references to God. The following paragraph is just a sample of how he referred to God. *"Now, sir, if this is founded in truth, I apprehend you will embrace every opportunity to eradicate that train of absurd and false ideas and opinions which so generally prevails with respect to us; and that your sentiments are concurrent with mine, which are that one Universal Father hath given being to us all; and that He hath not only made us all of one flesh, but that He hath also, without partiality, afforded us all the same sensations and endowed us all with the same faculties; and that however variable we may be in society or religion, however diversified in situation or color, we are all in the same family and stand in the same relation to Him. Sir, how pitiful is it to reflect that, although you were so fully convinced of the benevolence of the Father of Mankind and of His equal and impartial distribution of these rights and privileges which He hath conferred upon them, you should at the same time counteract His mercies in detaining by fraud and violence so numerous a part of my brethren under groaning captivity and cruel oppression, that you should at the same time be found guilty of that most criminal act, which you professedly detested in others, with respect to yourselves."*[17]

A Culture Out of Christianity

History reveals that our prayers, our faith in God, and our hard work have always been the key ingredients to our success as African Americans. This faith is evident in our historical archives, in our life-long struggles, and in our worship. God knew this, historians knew this, and James Weldon Johnson knew this as well. This is why he warned us not to *"stray from the God who has brought us thus far on our way"* (Jeremiah 3:21).

From the day we stepped onto American soil, blacks needed something and someone to guide them. This need was filled when the Bible became the constitution of our culture and the minister became the captain of our community—a captain who spoke for God. When he spoke everyone listened. In his book *Cosby,* author Dennis P. Eichhorn quotes actor Bill Cosby as saying, *"In our neighborhood, we never had an image to look up to aside from the minister."*[18] Cosby was right. The black minister became our first spiritual, political, and community leader. He emerged as a very powerful figure and played a significant role in the development of the African American culture.

Historian John Hope Franklin made the same point when he said, *"Many of the active leaders in the struggle against slavery came from the ranks of the Negro Clergymen."*[19] Included among them were powerful leaders such as Rev. Richard Allen and Rev. Absalom Jones. This remains true with our modern-day leaders as well, such as Bishop Charles H. Mason, Rev. Adam Clayton Powell, Rev. Andrew Young, Rev. Benjamin Hooks, Rev. Jesse Jackson, and, of course, the Rev. Dr. Martin Luther King, Jr. The black clergy was as powerful as an African chief and was revered as much as the African medicine man. Although he wore many hats, his primary job was to teach his people about the Word of God.

The clergy convinced blacks that the Bible was the inspired word of God. Blacks were told that God's word did not lie, it never changed, it was fair and consistent, but most of all, it would be the key to their success. The Bible became the black man's guide for living. It was inspiring, forthright, and contained many inspirational stories that mirrored our quest for freedom: Joseph saving his people from starvation, Moses bringing the Jews out of bondage, and Daniel being delivered from the lion's den, to name a few. The Bible told us how to raise our children, discipline our children, and protect our children. It instructed us to study, work hard, and to love our neighbors. And what was even more important, the Bible assured us *"If God was for us, who could be against us?"* (Romans 8:31).

Through the Holy Scripture, the black clergy taught African Americans the following:

1. To *"respect the clergy,"* using Romans 10:14-15, I Chronicles. 16:22, II Kings 2:23-25, I Timothy 5:17-18.

2. To *"be clean,"* using Exodus 19:10-14.

3. To **"trust God to solve our problems**," using a multitude of scriptures including Matthew 18:6, Phil. 4:13, Luke 18:7, Romans 12:9, Psalms 46:1, and Psalms 121:1-2.

4. To *"stand together,"* using Matthew 12:25, Eccl. 4:9-12, and Exodus 17:12.

5. To **"strive for peaceful solutions,"** using Matthew 5:44, Romans 12:18, and Hebrews 12:14.

6. To *"be a community by supporting one another through giving,"* using Acts 2:44-46-47 and Romans 15:25-27.

7. To **"work hard**," using Ecclesiastes 9:10 and II Thessalonians 3:8-11.

8. To *"love our families,"* using I Timothy 5:1-11, Ephesians 5:22-33, and Ephesians. 6:1-4.

9. To **"be law abiding,"** using scriptures such as Romans' 13th chapter and Titus 3:1.

10. To **"never compromise, to be bold and stand up for what you believe,"** using Daniel 3:16-18, Exodus' 7th chapter, and Acts 5:29.

According to Booker T. Washington, the Bible was the inspiration that motivated many to learn to read. Booker said, "*As fast*

*as any teacher could be secured, not only were day schools filled,
but night schools as well. The great ambition of the older people
was to try to learn to read the Bible before they died. With this
view in mind, men and women who were 50 and 75 years old would
be found in night schools. Day schools, night schools, and Sunday
schools were always crowded and often many had to be turned
away because there was no room."* [20]

The black church was everything. Besides providing spiritual
growth and guidance, the church was:

    a. an institution for training and development
    b. a political advocate for justice
    c. a support system for the family
    d. an educational institution for child development
    e. a builder of self-esteem
    f. a community resource for employment
    g. an organization for social activities
    h. an economic system for the poor
    i. a place to find a quality spouse
    j. an institution dedicated to building people of character

Professor Boyd-Franklin put it this way: *"Because of slavery
and segregation, the black church became a central force in the
lives of black people and evolved as the sole institution that
belonged entirely to the black community. The black church
became the multifunctional community institution. They often
established their own schools and Bible societies, serving the varied and widespread needs of a disenfranchised population. They
often were and still are one of the few places where black men and
women could feel that they were respected for their own talents
and abilities."* [21] Professor Franklin went on to say W.E.B. DuBois
*"Had shown the churches have provided an escape for black people
from their painful experiences."* [22]

A Faith-Based Race of People With Family Values

Before his death, Dr. Martin Luther King (in a *Playboy Maga-zine* interview) expressed his concerns regarding whether the church would maintain the role that it had played in the past. Propheti-cally, he stated the following:

> *"There are many signs that the judgment of God is upon the church as never before. Unless the early sacrificial spirit is recaptured, I am very much afraid that today's Christian church will lose its authenticity, forfeit the loyalty of millions, and we will see the Christian church dismissed as a social club with no meaning or effectiveness for our time, as a form without substance, as salt without savor. The real tragedy, though, is not Martin Luther King's disillusionment with the church, for I am sustained by its spiritual blessings as a min-ister of the gospel with a lifelong commitment; the real trag-edy is that in my travels, I meet young people of all races whose disenchantment with the church has soured into out-right disgust."*[23]

King's reference to the *"early sacrificial spirit"* refers to the previous role that the church had played in our lives and one that it should continue to assume today. It was during this period (1800 to 1960s) that African Americans evolved into a *faith-based* race of people with strong *family values*.

Unfortunately, today far too many people associate terms like "faith-based" and "family values" with the modern-day Republi-can Party. A careful study of Black History will reveal that living with *family values* or following a *faith-based* lifestyle are not new concepts to African Americans. To the African American, these terms represented more than a political theme; they represented a way of life. Our faith and our families were the two principal ingredients that brought us through slavery, oppression, and the horrors of institutional racism.

Over the years, our faith in God influenced everything we did. When white doctors refused to treat us, while the criminal justice system mistreated us, we called on God, activated our faith, and documented our experiences in song, singing, *"He* [God] *is our doctor in the sickroom and a lawyer in the courtroom."* "Faith" was merely a word in the Bible to most people, but to the African American, it was the basis for their survival.

The same can be said about the term "family values." From childhood, men were taught that the fate of their family was the man's responsibility. So when black men escaped from the plantation, many worked for several years just to save enough money to buy their family's freedom. If anyone can identify with being *faith-based* and having *family values*, it should be the African American. It was our faith in God that helped us to value our family's importance to a greater degree than most groups, because our situation was unlike any others.

Few people understood the importance of our relationship with God like James Weldon Johnson. That's why he wrote the words:

*"God of **our** weary years,*
*God of **our** silent tears.*
*Thou who hast brought **us** thus far on the way;*
Thou who hast by Thy might,
*Led **us** into the light,*
*Keep **us** forever in thy path, **we** pray.*
*Lest **our** feet stray from the places, **our** God,*
*where **we** met Thee,*
*Lest **our** hearts, drunk with the wine of the world,*
* **we** forget Thee.*
Shadowed beneath thy hand,
*May **we** forever stand,*
*True to **our** God,*
*True to **our** native land."*

When James Weldon Johnson wrote the words to the "Negro National Anthem," little did he know that, just over the horizon, processes called integration and desegregation would radically change our faith-based culture. African Americans not only integrated, they also assimilated and forgot their past. Many no longer put their faith in God, instead they put their faith in government and those representing government. The shift from God to government has resulted in behavior unheard-of and problems unprecedented. Things are not the same anymore. But this should be of no surprise; our demise was prophesied by both the prophet and the poet.

Chapter Two

Integration Not Assimilation

How Things Have Changed

Millions of Baby Boomers can recall sitting on porches or in living rooms listening to their parents and neighbors talk about the good old days when neighbors looked out for each other and when there was unity in the community. Communities where people often left their doors unlocked, even spanked their neighbor's children, and when almost everyone went to church on Sunday.

Now the Baby Boomers are telling their stories and a new generation is listening. After hearing how things were when his Baby Boomer parents were children, a child today would probably be inclined to write the following:

A Letter to Dr. Martin Luther King Jr.

Dear Dr. King;

"My name is Sean Conner, I'm twelve years old. You don't know me, but I heard a lot about you. My parents say things would be a lot different if you were still around.

Just last night on the news, it said that someone conducted a teacher's survey, and 70 percent of the teachers said they didn't know how to deal with a black child. School officials say that every forty-six seconds a black child drops out of school and that 32 percent of all children who are suspended from school are black. My mom and dad said it

19

wouldn't be this way if you were still around. They said you devoted much of your time fighting for equality in education.

My parents said you were a good man and that you were committed to strengthening the black family. They said when you were around, 52 percent of all black children lived in homes with two parents until they were seventeen years old. Now only 6 percent of black children remain in two-parent households till they reach age seventeen. My dad said before you left us, more black men were the heads of their household, but today over 55 percent of our households are headed by women and every eleven seconds a young black girl gives birth to her second child.

It seems like no one really cares about us anymore. We have more black politicians than ever before, but no one knows what they have done to make things better for black people. We see them on TV attending big social functions sponsored by their political parties, but Dad said we never see them in our community lending a helping hand like you used to do. I'm twelve, and I have never seen a black politician doing anything in my neighborhood. Dad said our leaders seem to be more concerned about the Confederate Flag in South Carolina than they are about our gang, drug, and teenage pregnancy problems.

My mother said she wishes you were still around because you stood for nonviolence. Since you left us, there has been a lot of violence in our community. Today, black children are no longer killed because they are the wrong color. They are killed simply because they are wearing the wrong color. Mom said things were much different when you were alive. She recalls during the summer months watching little children selling Kool-Aid and lemonade on the street corners in our neighborhood. Today, many of the corner Kool-Aid and lemonade stands are gone. The corners in a lot of neighborhoods have been taken over by drug dealers or have been the place of drive-by shootings. It's not the same anymore, Dr. King. Each day four black males are shot to death.

During one year 1,759 blacks were killed with guns and forty-five of them, were children under the age of ten. Some health experts say our people are dying at an alarming rate from violence and health-related conditions. One report said if we continue to die at this rate, only 2 percent of the black population will remain in America by the year 2150, but no one seems to care.

My dad said that when you were a civil rights leader, black men highly respected the African American woman. He said when Rosa Parks had a problem because they wouldn't let her sit in the front of the bus, you and other black men went down to Montgomery, Alabama, to help her. Dad said these were the times when black men used to call the women they loved sweet names like "honey," "baby," and "sugar." But now in music, movies, and TV programs, they refer to black women as "bitches" and "hos" and to blacks in general as "niggas." I don't know what some of these words mean. I just know that young black kids my age like to dance to music that use these types of lyrics and they like to attend movies where black actors and actress are required to use these words as part of the script. Daddy says movie makers and music producers make billions of dollars producing music and movies using scripts and lyrics that contain words like "bitches" and "hos" and most of their movies feature blacks killing blacks.

Not only have the names of black women changed, the names of black men have also changed. Dad said we used to refer to African American men as "brother" or "bro." But now they refer to them as dogs. Daddy said you would be very disappointed because you worked so hard to have black people respected and to rid our society of negative stereotypes about our people.

My mother said you spent a lot of time fighting for equal opportunity in employment so blacks could get better-paying jobs. But since you left us:

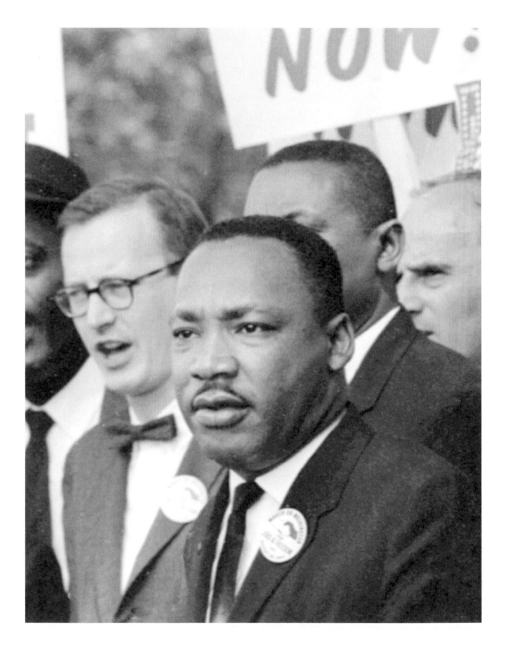

Rev. Dr. Martin Luther King Jr.
Things are different since he left us.

    a. *African American unemployment reached a record high of 21 percent.*

    b. *Unemployment among African American men is extremely high.*

    c. *Every ninety-five seconds, an African American child is born into poverty.*

Dr. King, they said if it weren't for you, there would probably be no Equal Opportunity Commission or Affirmative Action Programs. It's different now. Many states are abolishing Affirmative Action. Some insiders report that the Equal Opportunity Commission, which is supposed to protect women and minorities from employment discrimination, closes 95 percent of all discrimination complaints without even investigating them. Just before our last presidential election in 2000, we learned that the black Secret Service agents who protect the President filed a lawsuit against the Clinton administration for racial discrimination. In 1995 Mr. Clinton and his Justice Department defended a group of white janitors who claimed they were the victims of reverse discrimination. But in that same year, the President refused to help a group of black longshoremen in Seattle, Washington, who were denied promotions, and were forced to work in an environment where certain jobs were called "nigger jobs." Instead of punishing these companies who discriminated against the longshoremen, Mr. Clinton violated federal regulations by giving them millions of dollars in government contracts.

My mom was also upset with Jesse Jackson, the NAACP, and the Congressional Black Caucus because they didn't support the black longshoremen, nor did they condemn Clinton for giving the shipping companies the government contracts. My mom is pretty smart. She said the government is willing to spend thousands of dollars to keep a black man in jail, but they are not as willing to loan a black man the same amount to start a business or to go to college. She said none of this would be happening if you were still around.

Mother said you wouldn't care who was president, you would have stood up for the black longshoremen as well as the black Secret Service agents, just like you did for the black garbage workers in Memphis, Tennessee, just before you died.

My dad said you were a preacher and that it was you who got the black churches involved in the civil rights struggle to bring about social change. He said now that you are gone, the churches seem to have lost their interest in the struggle.

Dad said today churches are more concerned about their Sunday morning service than they are about their Monday morning service to their community. He said a lot of blacks no longer go to church and that many of the black clergy stood idly by while the government took prayer out of school. Mom said that would probably make you cry because you always prayed.

The last thing I heard them say about you was that you worked very hard to achieve racial equality and racial harmony. They said now that you are gone, no one is really concerned about hiding their racial prejudice. It seems like all of your efforts went up in smoke when the O.J. Simpson verdict came in—blacks felt one way, and whites felt another. Since you left us, people started burning black churches and Jewish synagogues again. We don't hear much about the Ku Klux Klan; they have been replaced with a group called "the skinheads." Dad said they are both the same, they just changed their uniforms from sheets to military outfits. Geraldo got into a fight with some on his TV show.

Dr. King, why did you leave us so soon? Why couldn't you have stayed around a little while longer? It is so unfair. My friends and I have never seen the times that my mom and dad talk about. It would have been nice to live in a community where there were two parents in practically every household and where families stuck together and supported each other; communities where people went to

church, prayed in schools, and loved each other; a commu-
nity where we called black men "brothers" and black women
"sisters"; a community where the churches were more con-
cerned with the services to their community rather than their
services on Sunday morning.

It's late. I have to go to bed now. My mom said I have to
get up early tomorrow because it will be a special day at
school. Tomorrow will be the first time we will have to wear
uniforms and go through a metal detector. The school
decided to do this after a classmate of mine shot and killed
another kid for wearing the wrong colors. Everybody misses
you so much, Dr. King. We wish you had never left us.
Love,
Sean Conner "

Integration: A Step Toward Assimilation

After reading Sean Conner's letter, one might ask, *"How did this happen and how did these changes come so soon without us realizing it?"* The facts cited in Sean's letter seem to suggest that a cultural evolution took place between his generation and his parents' generation. One generation lived during the period of segregation and the other during the period of integration.

In view of the contrast between the two different living experiences, one would have to ask: *"Is it a coincidence that, after integration, there was an increase in gang membership and a decrease in church membership, or that unemployment among black men increased while the number of black men heading households decreased? What caused this? How did this happen? Was integration the problem?"*

Most scholars will agree that the problem wasn't integration. The problem was the evolutionary process that took us from integration to *cultural assimilation.* Integration and cohabitation are the first phases of this process. Experts acknowledge that exposure to different and dominant cultures for an extended period of time will often result in assimilation. Integration has its benefits, but it also has its risks. One of those risks can include trading life-long cultural traditions for what the younger generation considers as modern ways. According to *Time* magazine reporter Eugene Linden, this happens with indigenous people when *"the young who are in contact with the outside world have embraced the view that traditional ways are illegitimate and irrelevant."*

Linden revealed his findings in a September 23, 1991, *Time* magazine article, entitled "Lost Tribes – Lost Knowledge." The article deals with two ways cultures have been destroyed: through property acquisition (under the name of modern development) and through cohabitation. Linden said, *"As the world's tribes are dying out or being absorbed into modern civilization, as they vanish so does their irreplaceable knowledge. Indigenous people have been threatened for centuries as development encroaches on their land and traditions. What is different about the present situation, however, is that it goes beyond basic questions of native land rights into more ambiguous issues, such as the prerogative of individuals to decide between traditional and modern ways. Indigenous knowledge disappears when natives are stripped of their lands, but in many parts of the globe, knowledge also disappears because **the young who are in contact with the outside world have embraced the view that traditional ways are illegitimate and irrelevant.**"*[24]

Most cultures today are not destroyed because of violent forceful takeovers by opposing nations. They are destroyed because their traditional ways and ideas are considered to be *illegitimate* and *irrelevant* by the stronger and more powerful culture. The process of cultural destruction enabled and expedited by cohabitation, is a long and gradual process, one that is achieved through a variety of changes. Such changes are caused and brought about by many factors, including: modern legislation, economic depredation, biased education, new trends, biased media, intimidation, racism, community destruction, and the loss of knowledge of traditional ways.

In his book, *Disuniting of America*, Harvard professor Arthur M. Schlesinger Jr. said, *"The first step in liquidating a people is to erase their memory. Destroy their culture and their history. Then have somebody write a new book, manufacture a new culture, and invent a new history. Before long they will begin to forget what it is and/or what it was."*[25]

What Art Schlesinger described in his book and *Time* magazine reporter Eugene Linden described in his article regarding cultural destruction is precisely what happened to the African American when we went beyond integration and cohabitation to assimilation. There is nothing wrong with integration in and of itself. The problem is this: Integration is usually followed by a process where groups and/or individuals find themselves losing or rejecting their own identity, values, and traditions and assuming those of the dominant culture. Experts call this process "assimilation."

Integration and desegregation came in the 1960s during a period when America was faced with a multitude of social changes. The traditional values that were once a part of the American mainstream were now being challenged and rejected by the Baby Boomers. History books were being rewritten; city, state, and federal governments were introducing a multitude of social programs designed to eliminate social injustices and racial prejudice. At the same time, radical groups were spreading new propaganda on college campuses all over America, propaganda that challenged the traditional way of living.

No one was ready for the sweeping changes and no one knew how these changes would affect the African American community. This was new territory for the African American. We had never faced such rapid social changes, nor were we aware of the possible negative impact that such changes would have on our culture. Most of us just held on and enjoyed the ride, not really knowing where it would take us. Most thought it would lead us to the **Promised Land of Equality**. We never thought it would lead us to the **Land of Lost Identity**.

The Struggle to Maintain Cultural Identity

Had we continued to study the Bible and the plight of the Jews, we would have been better prepared to deal with such changes. In Deuteronomy 6:10-17 and 18:9-14, the Lord instructs and warns the Jews not to assimilate when they moved into their new Promised Land. He lets them know that it would be harmful for them to take on the cultural traditions of others. He tells them that they must maintain their own cultural traditions because their cultural traditions are what works best for them (Deuteronomy 6:24).

Even today, the Jews continue to struggle with assimilation. Rabbi Halevy Doin, author of *To Raise A Jewish Child,* said: *"Today, raising a child to feel, think, and live the life of a Jew cannot be taken for granted. The environment in which most Jewish children are raised today differs radically from that which nurtured their parents and grandparents even if they were born and grew up in the United States. Many* [Jews] *judge the worth of their own religious faith on the basis of its compatibility with American principles and values, instead of assessing the worth of American values in terms of their own traditions. The Jew became so integrated into the life of America, so thoroughly had he absorbed the culture of this secular-Christian country, so accepted a citizen had he become in an atmosphere relatively free of anti-Semitism, and so little did he give expression of his own Jewish heritage, that the Jewish problem today is to undo the consequences of their own success in the great effort to become real Americans. In addition it cannot be denied that the rapidly changing mores of American society, increasingly conducive to the breakdown of family life, have also affected the Jewish life. Jewish influence on the spiritual history of mankind has always been the greatest when Jews were true to themselves and to their own heritage. The Judaization of the Jew, consistent with traditional values, will provide the Jew with the means by which to overcome those problems of the spirit that engulf Western Society. It*

*will serve to give our children not only what they need to live with,
but what to live for."*[26]

Sarah Silberstein Swartz explains how the Jews have traditionally passed on their cultural traditions to the next generation. In her
book, *Bar Mitzvah*, she writes: *"A* [Jewish] *boy is first taught the
Hebrew alphabet at the age of three, studies the Bible at the age of
five, and learns rabbinical commentaries at the age of ten. He is
taken to the synagogue on a regular basis by age four, and, from
then on, is formally educated in the Jewish culture and values."*[27]

Forsaking Religious Values for Social Acceptance

The traditional practices of the Jews were quite similar to the
traditional practices of African Americans during the post desegregation period. Like the Jews, we taught our children our history,
we established our cultural and family traditions, and we took our
children to church on the weekends.

By the 1970s, integration and desegregation had started to take
its toll on our culture. School textbooks had been rewritten to
include more black history and some of the social programs that
were once a part of the social structure of the church were now
being sponsored by the government. With the new government
social programs, many felt they no longer needed the church. Black
historian John Hope Franklin said that by the 1970s, church membership among blacks had started to decline.

Christianity Today magazine reported in their March 4, 1996,
article on the "Black Church" *"A generation ago, 80% of blacks
went to church. Today that figure is 40%."* Cain Hope Felder,
professor of New Testament at Howard University School of
Divinity in Washington, D.C., laments, *"Many black churches
offer meaningless religiosity that let people off the hook and is
seen by many as the priest of the status quo."*[28]

Some blacks left the church because they felt they no longer
needed the church; others left because they claimed that they could

no longer identify with the Christian faith, nor were they comfortable worshipping what they referred to as "a white man's God." Many of these individuals turned to Islam. They did so without realizing that it was the Muslims who sold our people into slavery 800 years before America was discovered. According to the *Encyclopedia Britannica*, approximately 18,000,000 Africans were enslaved by Islamic countries from 650 AD to 1905.[29] While many blacks turned their backs on the traditional black church and embraced the Muslim faith, others were gradually influenced and absorbed by the dominant culture around them.

The process of assimilation had begun, and the cultural traditions African Americans were once accustomed to had started to dissipate. William Turner, Director of Black Church Affairs at Duke University Divinity School at Durham, North Carolina, said: "*Many of the black churches have changed and now define success out of American Corporate reality. That definition includes: fancy cars, itinerant executives, and corporate careers, like many white churches.*"[30]

In an interview with *Christianity Today*, Jawanza Kunjufu, author of *Counter the Conspiracy to Destroy Black Boys*, says: "*80-90 percent of the 37,000 black churches are more about entertainment (singing, shouting, and hollering) and keeping their doors open on Sunday than they are about empowering the community.*" He suggests that black churches should first "*Teach who Jesus is, and second, empower the community*" if they are going to get blacks to return to the church.[31]

Things were happening just as Arthur Schslesinger Jr. had predicted. He said the first step in eliminating a people was to destroy their culture, then create a new history, and before long they would forget who they were and what it [their history] was. When black history was rewritten by modern-day text book writers, they deliberately left out the God who was the foundation and inspiration behind our history.

For instance, when modern-day historians wrote the story about Jackie Robinson, the first black to enter into major league baseball,

Jackie Robinson
The first African American to play in Major League Baseball, he
was selected because of his baseball skills *and* his faith in God.

they failed to mention that it was Jackie's relationship with God that convinced general manager Branch Rickey of the Brooklyn Dodgers that he was the right man to break the color line. Jackie wasn't selected because he was the best player in the Negro Baseball League. Many protested his selection, arguing that Satchel Paige and Josh Gibson were much better ball players. In fact, according to Bruce Chapwick, author of *When the Game Was Black and White*, Jackie wasn't even the best player on the Kansas City Monarchs, the team he played for in the Negro League. Chapwick said: "*Oftentimes Jackie sat on the bench during many games while better players played.*"[32]

Branch Rickey wasn't looking for Jackie to break the color line. He was looking for Jackie's faith in God to break the color line. Some say Rickey advised Jackie to think about "*what Jesus would do*" any time he encountered a racist situations on the field. The role that Jackie's faith played in the breaking of the color line was deliberately omitted from most history books.

In writing about some of our other great leaders, frequently the historians omitted their title of "Reverend" and mentioned them by their name only. Seldom did they ever mention the role that the black church played in the development of our people and our culture. Most historians, both black and white, never mention how much our historical figures prayed and relied on God for their success.

When the new history books were completed, our old culture, which recognized the role God had played in our history, was virtually deleted. As a result, blacks began to protest more than we prayed. We griped more than we were grateful. And we focused more on **feeling** good rather than **being** good. We embraced the **melting pot** philosophy more than the **garden salad** concept, where each vegetable maintains its own identity while being a part of the whole salad. When we stepped out of this so-called melting pot, we had dissolved into something else and could not recognize ourselves. We were born again (a new creation), but not in the spiritual sense. We were newborn babes in a new changing secular society. Our old identity had melted away. With many, NFL football or a round of golf replaced Sunday morning worship, drugs took the place of divine guidance, and our faith in God was replaced with our faith in government programming.

Like the Jews, African Americans were so eager to be socially accepted in clubs, neighborhoods, schools, and occupations from which they were traditionally excluded, they unconsciously traded important cultural values and traditions for social acceptance. We thought we had entered the **Promised Land**. Instead we had entered into a **Land of Unhealthy Practices**. We strayed away from our cultural identity, violated God's principles, and took on the destructive and ungodly ways of our secular society (Deuteronomy. 6:24). Many blacks, particularly the older blacks, believe we were better off before we entered the era of integration. Older blacks are convinced that before integration African Americans had:

1. A higher percentage of two-parent families and lower percentage of single-parent families.
2. A higher percentage of those who were joined together in holy wedlock and a lower percentage of couples living together out of wedlock.
3. A higher percentage of people who trusted in God and a lower percentage of people who put their trust in government.
4. A higher percentage of those who were employed and a lower percentage of those who were in prison.
5. A higher percentage of those who supported black businesses and a lower percentage of those who ignored black businesses.
6. A higher percentage of those who depended on Christ and a lower percentage of those who depended on crack.
7. A higher percentage of teens who respected their parents and a lower percentage of teens who themselves were parents.
8. A higher percentage of children born from wedlock and a lower percentage of children born out of wedlock.
9. A higher percentage of those who cherished life and a lower percentage of those who took their life.

10. A higher percentage of those who supported each other and a lower percentage of people who killed one another.
11. A higher percentage of families that spanked their children and lower percentage of families that neglected their children.
12. A higher percentage of children in churches and a lower percentage of children in jails.
13. A higher percentage of teens who respected our property and lower percentage of teens who destroyed our property.
14. A higher percentage of children doing well in school and a lower percentage of children who failed in school.
15. A higher percentage of children carrying books to schools and a lower percentage of children carrying guns to school.
16. A higher percentage of teens who were members of the church and a lower percentage of teens who were members of gangs.
17. A higher percentage of marriages within our race and a lower percentage of marriages outside our race.
18. A higher percentage of songs expressing our love for our women and a lower percentage of songs degrading our women.

No other group in history has suffered more than the blacks and the Jews. Neither has any other group so willingly abandoned its cultural identity to be socially accepted. Many felt that our true cultural identity was tied to the mother continent of Africa, so we started wearing Afro hairstyles and African attire. Little did we know that our true cultural identity was never really tied to Africa, but rather to the God who made Africa.

People will often sell, trade, or relinquish something of value when they are unaware of its true worth. In the Bible, Esau traded his birthright for a bowl of soup, Judas traded Jesus for thirty pieces of silver and while traveling down the road to integration, blacks traded their godly culture for social acceptance without realizing that what they gave up was priceless.

Chapter Three

The Hard Choice: Government or God

During the period of integration, both the people and the preacher looked to the government for answers. With African Americans and women in mind, the government responded with a multitude of social programs to correct racial and gender discrimination, as well as programs to address the social conditions of the poor. Among those included were:

1. Affirmative Action Programs
2. Special employment training for minorities and women
3. Set-aside government contracts for minorities and women
4. Open housing programs to integrate neighborhoods
5. School busing programs to integrate schools
6. Summer job programs for inner-city youth
7. Neighborhood matching grants for inner-city programs
8. Special college entrance programs for minorities and women
9. Special college programs for women in sports
10. Sex education classes
11. Needle exchange programs for drug users
12. Free condoms for sexually active youth
13. Government-sanctioned abortions
14. Government housing units for the low-income earners

15. Programs to register more black voters
16. Headstart programs for small children

The Upside of Social Changes

After almost forty years of government programming, there are mixed reviews regarding their effectiveness. On one hand we have the following:

1. More middle-class blacks
2. More ethnic minorities and women in nontraditional jobs
3. More minority- and women-owned businesses
4. More women in college sports
5. More African Americans attending college
6. More teens working
7. More grants given to black churches for social programs
8. More black and female politicians
9. More black voters

The Downside of Social Changes

On the other hand we have:

1. More homeless than ever before
2. More rat- and roach-infested government housing
3. Fewer mothers who are full-time homemakers
4. More latchkey children home alone
5. More violence in our schools
6. More daycare programs caring for our children
7. More couples living together out of wedlock
8. More single mothers who have never been married
9. More covert practices of racial discrimination
10. More hate groups like the neo-nazi skinheads

11. More black church burnings
12. More black men unemployed than ever before
13. More African American youth in the juvenile justice system
14. More black men in prison
15. More black men with longer sentences than their white counterparts
16. More pregnancies among black teens
17. More abortions among black women
18. More sexually transmitted diseases among blacks, including AIDS
19. More blacks in gangs than ever before
20. More drugs in the black community
21. More gang violence in black communities
22. More gang-related violence in inner-city schools
23. More black on black crime
24. More violent deaths among blacks aged 15 to19
25. More top-40 music degrading black women and glorifying sex and violence
26. More single-parent households headed by African American women
27. More black men absent in African American households
28. More blacks who do not believe in God nor go to church

God's Track Record Vs Government Programs

What happened? Why the negative results? Through modern-day leadership, both inside and outside the black community, the government was convinced that if they could change the social conditions of the people, they could change the behavioral lifestyles of the people. How effective was the government in changing behavior? Contrary to what many may have believed, the evidence will show that the government has never been as effective as the Christian church in the area of behavioral modification and character development. The facts will show that the Christian church has converted more gang members, drug dealers, and hardcore criminals than any government institution or any government-sponsored program. Harvard economist Richard Freeman told *Christianity Today* magazine, *"Church attendance was the best predictor of which young inner city black males were likely to escape the syndrome of gangs, drugs, and prison."*[33]

The article goes on to say, *"Churches have an advantage over most government and secular programs because:*

1. *They have a semi-organized pool of volunteers.*
2. *During the week, they provide physical space.*
3. *They can raise discretionary funds for the needy (with an average income of $36 billion a year).*
4. *They have a place and authority to assemble the community for discussion.*
5. *They have the potential for political influence.*
6. *They offer moral authority and evidence that people can leave behind destructive behavior.*
7. *They provide a sense of family that can be a substitute for dysfunctional family life.*
8. *They have links to a larger community that can offer jobs, resources, and political influence.*
9. *And finally, churches are present almost everywhere. This is particularly true in the inner-city neighborhoods where every other institution has failed or disappeared, but the church."*

Reporters for *Newsweek* magazine seem to agree. In a June 1, 1998, *Newsweek* article entitled "God Vs Gangs," with a subtitle of "What's the Hottest Idea in Crime Fighting? The Power of Religion," the magazine states:

"For decades, liberals and conservatives have argued about the crisis in the inner city. The right was obsessed with crime,

out-of-wedlock births, and the responsibility of the underclass. The
left only wanted to talk about poverty, the need for government
intervention, and the rights of the poor.

"Now both sides are beginning to form an unlikely alliance
founded on the idea that the only institution with the spiritual
message and the physical presence to rescue kids from the seduc-
tions of drugs and gangs while instilling the much-needed tradi-
tional values is the church."[34]

The conclusions of the liberals and the conservatives are
correct. It was God, not a government program, that changed Paul,
a well-known Pacific Islander drug dealer from the inner city who
experienced both the pain and prosperity of the drug business. Four
years ago, when Paul wanted to make a change, he didn't turn to a
government program, but to the inner-city church. Today he serves
as a youth pastor for Mt. Calvary Christian Center Church of God
in Christ and assists his wife with her daycare business.

Dee dropped out of high school at the age thirteen and became
a teenage mother at nineteen. Selling drugs was her only child
support. After being shot and prosecuted for drug possession, she
was ordered to attend a government-sponsored program for troubled
teens called Job Corps. Upon graduation, she took the money that
she had earned from that government program and bought more
drugs to reactivate her drug business. When she really wanted to
change her life, she, like Paul, turned to the church, not to a government program. Two years ago Dee graduated from college with
a degree in marketing and has a marketing support job in the
research department of a major newspaper. When she is not devot-
ing her time to her eight-year-old son, she works with the church
and inner-city teens.

It was God, not a government program that changed Ben, a
young man from Detroit who tried to stab another young man his
age. After establishing a relationship with God, young Ben went
on to complete college and medical school. Today he no longer
uses a knife as a weapon to hurt others, but as a tool to help others.
This former problem child from the inner city now holds over

twenty-six honorary doctorate degrees and is the professor of Neurosurgery, Plastic Surgery, and Oncology as well as an assistant professor of Pediatrics at John Hopkins University School of Medicine. Dr. Benjamin Solomon Carson, who was raised by a single parent, is currently the Director of Pediatric Neurosurgery at the Johns Hopkins University Hospital. In 1987, he made headlines when he served as the lead surgeon of a seventy-member medical team that successfully separated seven-month-old German twins who were joined together at the backs of their heads.

These individuals represent hundreds of thousands of supposedly unreachable inner-city young people whose lives have been transformed by the Christian church.

There are a number of differences between God's program and the government's program. What are they? God does not depend on votes and taxes to accomplish His task, nor is He afraid of being voted out of office. Therefore, He is free to do what is necessary to bring about the much-needed changes. Public opinion does not sway Him, Congress cannot stop Him, and no military force on earth can defeat Him. He *"walks with kings and keeps His virtue and talks with men and never loses the common touch"* (Kipling). God's affirmative action program touches the lives of every person, both rich and poor, black and white. You cannot influence Him with earthly money, prestige, or power. Instead, He is influenced by a broken heart and a simple sincere prayer. There are many things that the government cannot do, but with God, *"all things are possible"* (Matthew 19:26).

Former Congressman Floyd Flake, and author of *The Way of the Bootstrapper,* said it best when he said. *"I believe that a large number of a bootstrapper's successes are attributable to the individual's investment of time, energy, and resources. I also believe that, without God, none of it would be possible."*[35] In other words, whatever we do to address our problems, God must be part of the solution if we want long-lasting effective results. Apparently, President George W. Bush also feels this way. When the terrorists attacked New York and the Pentagon on September 11, 2001, the

Dr. Ben Carson
A former angry kid from the inner-city,
who now uses his knife to help others.

President didn't look to Congress for wisdom to deal with this horrific problem. He looked to God and asked the entire nation to pray.

Legislation Without Spiritual Transformation

For forty years we looked to the government to do things that
it really had no power to do. Throughout this period we learned
that government programs may or may not produce better opportunities, but they cannot produce better people. We learned that legislation without spiritual transformation cannot change people for
the better. And finally, we learned that it is wiser to put our trust in
God rather than in the government, because the government cannot do what God can do.

Our American currency tells us to **trust in God**, our Bible
tells us to **trust in God**, and the old-time black preacher told us to
trust in God. Yet somewhere along the way, we were convinced
that the government could do what God could not. Historically,
this is contrary to what African Americans were taught. To return
to our original values, those that have sustained us throughout history, we must once again focus on the God who is the "*author and
finisher of faith*" (Hebrews 12:2) along with the compelling Scriptures that inspired us. Scriptures such as:
Acts 5:29
"We ought to obey God rather than man."
Matthew 19:26
"With men it is impossible but with God all things are possible."
Psalms 127:1 (NIV)
*"Unless the Lord builds the house, its builder's labor is in vain. Unless
the Lord watches over the city, the watchmen stand guard in vain."*
Romans 8:3
*"For what the law could not do, in that it was weak through the flesh,
God sending his own Son in the likeness of sinful flesh, and for sin,
condemned sin in the flesh."*

By both sermon and songs, church leaders reminded African Americans to keep trusting in God and to *"look to the hills, from whence cometh our help."* They told us, *"our help comes from God who made the heavens and earth"* (Psalms 121:1-2). Black churches sang many hymns and spiritual songs, but none as popular as "I will trust in the Lord till I die" and "The Lord Will Make a Way Somehow." They would sing these songs until tears rolled down their cheeks. The songs gave them joy in sorrow, hope for tomorrow, and peace in the midst of confusion.

When the old-time preacher would teach on Romans 8:3, he would tell the congregation that laws are only as good as the people who are in charge of them. So if the person is corrupt, the law will be corrupt. If the person is weak, the law will be weak. If the person is prejudiced, the outcome will be prejudice. The preacher told us that laws change but God never changes nor does His law. He told us, *"God is the same today, yesterday, and will be forever. For this cause you can trust God, but you can never fully trust man."*

The Winans (a Grammy Award winning gospel group) put it this way in their song "Right Left in a Wrong World":

> *"I can't trust in a political system,*
> *The world is so rough that it's cold.*
> *I can trust in Your [Jesus] very existence*
> *You're the only thing right,*
> *Left in a wrong world."*

By the 1960s, many African Americans were no longer listening to biblical messages from our ministers. Instead, they turned their focus to the political propaganda from our preachers and many of our preachers told us to vote Democrat, so we did. By the mid-sixties many blacks started to trust government more and God less and became more *loyal* to the Democratic Party than to God's divine promises. But to chart the beginning of this love affair between blacks and Democrats, we have to travel back to the 1920s.

Chapter Four

The Switch from Republican to Democrat

In 1929, one year after President Herbert Hoover took office with a promise to *"put a chicken in every pot,"* the stock market crashed, our nation went into a deep depression, and the Republicans knew they were in trouble. This was the perfect opportunity for the Democrats to take the White House, but they needed more than the Depression; they needed the black vote. During this same period, several black newspapers, including the *Baltimore Afro-American*, the *Norfolk Journal,* and the *Pittsburgh Courier* had become very critical of the Republican Party. As their collective circulation soared into the millions, these newspapers became a very powerful voice in the black community.

Prior to this time from 1866 to 1928, blacks had voted exclusively for the Republican ticket. Frustrated with the economy as well as with the Republican Party, the newspapers used their powerful voice to urge black voters to break tradition and vote Democrat. John Hope Franklin said, *"The break was neither clean nor complete, however, for there were those who could not be persuaded to support the party that, after all, was the party of the Ku Klux Klan and other bigots."*[36]

On Election Day in 1933, the collective voices of the newspapers were heard and when the votes were counted, Democratic candidate Franklin D. Roosevelt was the new President of the United States. Blacks didn't switch parties because of the hard times

brought about by the *Depression*. Hard times were nothing new
for the American Negro. They voted Democrat because the *Pittsburgh Courier* and other powerful black newspapers told their readers the *"Republicans took their vote for granted."*

Roosevelt continued to court the black vote by inviting
Negroes to the White House, appointing several to serve on various commissions and placing many more on the federal payroll.
Black employment in federal jobs increased from 50,000 to 200,000,
but Roosevelt developed no specific programs to address the problems facing African Americans.

Professor John Hope Franklin said, *"The benefit that Negroes
received from Franklin's New Deal **was not** the result of the formu-
lation of **specific** programs for them. Rather, it came from their
being the logical beneficiaries of programs designed to help the
poor and disadvantaged, of whatever race. They* [blacks] *discovered, however, that agencies of the federal government were as
capable of discriminatory practices, or could be used for such purposes, as any others. Black sharecroppers and tenants had difficulty in obtaining relief benefits from the Agricultural
administration because landlords kept their relief checks. While
the Federal Housing Authority guaranteed a limited number of
loans for Negroes to build or purchase homes, its policy was not to
interfere with local housing practices that excluded Negroes from
certain neighborhoods. Lynchings and other forms of racial violence had continued during the New Deal and the federal government had pleaded that it had no jurisdiction over such matters."*[37]

Twenty years later, after blacks had voted for two Democratic
administrations, our military bases at home were still segregated,
our request for a permanent Civil Rights Commission was still
denied, and the living conditions of African Americans were still
deplorable. This sparked the new Civil Rights Movement of the
1950s and 1960s. During the height of the movement, black newspapers were no longer the powerful voice that they once were, and
African Americans were more inclined to listen to their preacher than
to their newspaper publisher. After Eisenhower took 40 percent of

the black vote in 1952, the black vote was again up for grabs when his term finally ended in 1960.

Promises from politicians in the sixties convinced a new generation of African Americans that the government had the answers to employment discrimination, poverty, and racial injustices. Candidates from the Democratic Party told black preachers and their newly registered voters that, if they voted for the Democrats, they would pass legislation and develop programs that would address the concerns of African Americans. While many younger blacks were willing to give the Democrats their votes, some of the older blacks who knew their history were reluctant and skeptical. What did they know?

1. They knew that although Franklin D. Roosevelt and Harry S. Truman were nice men who ended segregation in the military *overseas* and had set up various commissions to look into racial discrimination, neither had passed any *major* civil rights legislation to address the overall problems of blacks.

2. They knew that under the Roosevelt/Truman administrations, anti-lynching laws were rejected as well as efforts to establish a permanent Civil Rights Commission. During these administrations, black soldiers could no longer read outspoken Negro newspapers like the *Pittsburgh Courier*, as they were considered communist and were banned from the military by the Roosevelt administration, even though these were the very same newspapers that gave Roosevelt the black vote and the White House.

3. They knew it was the Democratic Party who fought to keep blacks in bondage.

4. They knew that the Republican Party was the first major political party that openly expressed their opposition to slavery and took a firm position against it.

5. They knew that it was the Republican Party who pushed and fought for their emancipation.

6. They knew that from 1869 to 1880 there were sixteen black men who served in the United States Congress, and they were all members of the Republican Party.

7. They knew that during Reconstruction (1867-1877), Hiram Revels and Blanche K. Bruce both served as United States Senators. They were black and members of the Republican Party. (See Appendix E)

8. They knew that the Democratic Party had never elected a black man to serve in the United States Senate. (See Appendix E)

9. They knew that it was the Republicans and the Abolitionists many of whom were also Republicans who moved South and pushed for changes in the law after slavery had ended.

10. They knew that the Civil Rights Acts of 1866 and 1875 were both passed by Republican administrations.

11. They also knew that the Thirteenth, Fourteenth, and Fifteenth Amendments granting blacks freedom, citizenship, and the right to vote were all passed by Republican administrations.

12. They knew that Eisenhower and the Republicans went beyond integration in the military and passed both the

1957 Civil Rights Act, the Civil Rights Act of 1960, and sent U.S. troops to Arkansas to desegregate schools.

13. They knew every piece of legislation designed to make blacks second-class citizens or to take away blacks' rights as citizens was the proud work of the Democrats.

14. They knew that it was the Democrats who sponsored and passed Black Codes and Jim Crow laws, which legalized a multitude of discriminatory practices designed to deny blacks their rights as citizens.

15. They knew that had it been left up to the Democrats, blacks would still be slaves and slavery would be practiced in every new Northern state.

16. They knew that all of our key historical figures identified with the Republican Party, including Frederick Douglass, Harriet Tubman, Sojourner Truth, and Booker T. Washington, and that prior to the 1930s, blacks in general voted Republican.

After giving Roosevelt and Truman their votes in the thirties and forties with very little show for it, blacks were again asked to give the Democrats their vote in the sixties. Many couldn't understand how the Democrats could ask for their vote without apologizing for their past and more recent racist practices under Roosevelt and Truman. Many quietly asked themselves: *"How could these people completely ignore their past sins and their inhumane treatment of our people and ask for our vote without shame or remorse?"*

Learning of History Before the Final Switch

The 1960s were turbulent times. They were times of irreversible social changes ignited by riots, civil rights protests, voter registration, and a search for positive identity. It was a time when blacks learned of their rich African American heritage and it was a time when they became *black and proud*. The learning process revealed many aspects of their history that few had ever talked about.

Blacks had a new image, a new attitude, and new books that highlighted portions of their history that were shocking and revealing. The books showed graphic pictures of slaves packed on ships like sardines, lying in their own urine and feces; told stories of how our women were raped, our men beaten and hanged; and explained how our families were divided and sold to other plantations.

After being exposed to the true role Democrats played in our history, many blacks were confused. They knew that almost a century ago, members of the Democratic Party gave their lives to keep us in bondage and now they wanted us to give them our vote to keep them in office. Some called it *"The Civil War"* and others called it *"The War Between the States,"* but our great-grandparents knew it as the war between the Democrats and the Republicans regarding the issue of slavery. The Republicans fought to **ban it** and the Democrats fought to **expand it**.

Whether on the battlefield or on the Senate floor, the Democratic party felt so strongly about their right to own our people that they were willing to engage in fist fights or any other violence to defend what they believed in. In his book, *Senator Charles Sumner*, Harvard history professor David Herbert Donald tells of a fight that took place on the U.S. Senate floor on May 21, 1856. After hearing a fiery speech condemning slavery by Republican Senator Charles Sumner, Preston Brooks, a Democratic Congressman from South Carolina, crept up behind Sumner and attacked him with a walking cane. When Preston knocked Sumner to the floor, several Republicans came to Sumner's rescue. The Democrats retaliated

Senator Charles Sumner
He was nearly beaten to death on the Senate floor because
of his speech opposing slavery.

on behalf of Brooks and the Senate brawl was on, Democrats and Republicans in a fist fight on the Senate floor. Professor Donald gave the following account of what happened after the dust settled:

"While Brooks was being led off, Sumner partially supported by Morgan, lay at the side of the center aisle, his feet in the aisle, and he leaning partially against a chair. He remained senseless as a corpse for several minutes, his head bleeding copiously from the frightful wounds, and the blood saturating his clothes. Dr. Cornelius Boyle, who had been hastily summoned, dressed the wounds, which were still bleeding profusely, and put two stitches in each. Sumner's shirt around the neck and collar was soaked with blood. The waistcoat had many marks of blood upon it; also the trousers. The broadcloth coat was covered with blood on the shoulders so thickly that the blood had soaked through the cloth, even through the padding, and appeared on the inside; there was also a great deal of blood on the back of the coat and its sides... [At the hospital] Before falling into a dazed sleep, Sumner remarked: 'I could not believe that a thing like this was possible.'

Arrested on a charge of assault, Brooks was immediately freed under a $500 bail and became the hero of the extreme pro-slavery clique. Armed and menacing, Southern fire-eaters talked of imitating Brook's example and made violent threats against other Northern leaders. [Saying] It would not take much to have the throats of every Abolitionist cut. If the Northern men had stood up, the city would now float with blood. And if Congress dared to discuss Brooks' actions, the House of Representatives would ring vollies [sic] from revolvers."[38]

The Sixties: Which Party Gets the Black Vote?

Although most of the older blacks knew nothing about the Sumner incident, they and their grandparents were very familiar with what took place during their lifetime in a democratic controlled South:

beatings, lynchings, and countless murders. They also knew that it was the Democrats who gave their lives to keep us as slaves while the Radical Republicans gave their lives to free us as slaves. The younger generation, those with college degrees, knew this as well, but they found it very difficult to understand why the Republicans, who were responsible for the Emancipation Proclamation and the four Civil Rights Acts (1866, 1875, 1957, and 1960) seemed reluctant and hesitant about eliminating all forms of racial discrimination. They felt that in the 1950s Eisenhower was pressured to send troops to Arkansas when faced with matters of desegregation and if he was apprehensive in enforcing his own desegregation laws, what would his Republican successor, Richard Nixon, do?

During their college studies, the younger generation received a vast amount of information that the older generation did not have. For instance, they learned that Lincoln was forced to do what he did for blacks by Radical Republicans. Their professors exposed them to various speeches that Lincoln had made during his lifetime, including one during his fourth debate with Stephen Douglas in 1858. Lincoln told his potential voters:

"I will say then that I am not, nor have ever been, in favor of bringing about in any way the social and political equality of the white and black races, [applause] that I am not, nor ever been, in favor of making voters or jurors of Negroes, nor of qualifying them to hold office, nor to intermarry with white people. And I will say in addition to this that there is a physical difference between the white and black races, which I believe will forever forbid the two races living together on terms of social and political equality. And inasmuch as they cannot so live, while they do remain together there must be the position of superior and inferior, and I as much as any other man am in favor of having the superior position assigned to the white race."[39]

Not only did Lincoln feel blacks were inferior to whites, he also had difficulty reaching a decision on the slavery issue. Political science professor, Malcolm Moos of Johns Hopkins University, said:
"Lincoln himself, who was to emerge as the greatest Republican

President Abraham Lincoln
The 16th President of the United States believed whites were superior
to blacks.

Party leader of all time, was not yet committed to the opposition of slavery, and in fact was openly critical of the tactics of the abolitionists. "[40]

On August 22, 1862, in response to a manifesto entitled *Prayer of Twenty Millions*, written by Horace Greeley and published by the *New York Tribune*, Lincoln said: "*My paramount object in this struggle is to save the Union and is not either to save or destroy slavery. If I could save the union without freeing any slave, I would do it. If I could save it by freeing all slaves, I would do that. If I could free it by freeing some and leaving others alone, I would do that also. What I do about slavery and the colored race, I do because I believe it helps save the Union.* "[41]

Historians say that as Lincoln and certain members of the Republican Party continued to vacillate on the issue of slavery and on the issue of racial superiority, Radical Republicans and their Abolitionist supporters stood firm and forced them to comply.

Professor James McPherson of Princeton University said: "*The abolitionists became the respected spokesmen for the radical wing of the Republican Party.*"[42] Among the radicals was William H. Herndon, Lincoln's Illinois law partner. On December 10, 1860, he wrote the following letter to the Republican Party:

> "*I am thoroughly convinced that two such civilizations as the North and the South cannot co-exist on the same soil and be co-equal in the Federal Brotherhood. To expect otherwise would be to expect the Absolute to sleep with and tolerate **hell**.*
>
> *I helped to make the Republican Party, and if it forsakes its distinctive ideas, I can help to tear it down and help erect a new party that shall never cower to any slave driver. Let this natural war, let this inevitable struggle proceed on, till slavery is **dead, dead, dead.**"*[43]

Herndon's threat had an impact. From 1861 to 1960 the Republicans dominated the office of the presidency. Prior to 1861, when there was only one party to speak of besides the Whigs, the

Democrats dominated the office. See Appendix A for a list of U.S. Presidents.

College Students Learn Democrats Terrorize Blacks to Force Blacks to Vote Democrat

Following Herndon's powerful threat, the Republicans fought hard and were successful in bringing about the Emancipation Proclamation. But our problems didn't end after the Proclamation was signed. History tells us that the high expectations blacks had after the Proclamation was signed soon disappeared in a Democrat-controlled South.

During Reconstruction, African Americans were beaten, lynched, and denied voting rights, and they experienced discrimination in housing, education, and employment. Blacks had problems in both the North and the South. However, the problems in the South were beyond comparison. In 1863, blacks were free according to the Emancipation Proclamation, but not free from the terrorist attacks by the Democrats and their Klan supporters. Some may feel that the word "terrorist" is a very strong word to use. However, after reading this entire fact-finding investigation, you may have a different opinion. In 1888, Rev. Ernest Lyons and colleagues from Louisiana used the following words to describe what they were experiencing. Rev. Lyons said, "*...a reign of **terror** exists in many parts of our states.*" (See Introduction for the complete letter.) See Appendix H 1898-1940 and Appendix I.

Professor John Hope Franklin wrote, "*...the Democrats resorted to violence*" just to stay in power. "*In some communities Negroes were forced to vote for Democrats.*" However some blacks fought back. "*During the elections of 1892, riots broke out in Virginia and North Carolina,*" Franklin reported. "*If Negro rule meant chaos and disorder to the Democrats, the mere threat of it was enough for the **Democrats** to resort to violence themselves.*

*As early as 1866 when Southern whites had almost complete charge of Reconstruction, a kind of **guerrilla warfare** was carried out against both blacks and whites who represented the Washington government in the South. These white Southerners, who were determined to guide their own destiny and control Negroes, struck with fury and rage."*[44]

In 1871, several Southern blacks were interviewed regarding their voting preferences and the intimidation that they experienced at the polls. The interviews were documented by the *Joint Select Committee to Inquire Into Conditions of Affairs in the Late Insurrectionary States*. The interviews became a part of *Senate Report No. 579* in the 48th Congress.

On November 1, 1871, John Childers of Livingston, Alabama, was interviewed by the Select Committee. The following is a portion of his interview as documented by Herbert Aptheker in his book, *Documentary History of the Negro People in the United States Vol. 2*:

Question: *Did you ever hear any threats made by Democrats against Negroes of what would be done* [to him] *if he voted the radical* [meaning Republican] *ticket?*

Answer: *I have had threats on myself. I can tell them.*

Question: *What kind of threats were made to you?*

Answer: *I have had threats that if we all would vote the Democratic ticket we would be well thought of, and the white men of the county—the old citizens of the county—would protect us; and every struggle or trouble we got into we could apply to them for protection, and they would assist us.*

Question: *Where did you hear that said?*

Answer: *I have heard it often. At the last election it was given to me. There was a man standing here in the courthouse door; when I started to the ballot box he told me he had a coffin already made for me, because he thought I was going to vote the radical* [meaning Republican] *ticket.*

Question: *Who was that man?*

Answer: *Well, I am afraid to tell his name, sir.*

Question: *Were the colored folks generally alarmed by these threats and afraid to vote their true sentiments?*

Answer: *Yes sir, they were.*

Question: *I have heard that a great many colored people voted the Democratic ticket at the last governor's election.* [Is that true?]

Answer: *Yes, sir.*

Question: *What made them do it?*

Answer: *For fear. I voted myself. I voted the Democratic ticket.*

Question: *Were you afraid if you voted the radical ticket you would be harmed?*

Answer: *I was, sir, because as I just stated to you, there was a man that told me he had a coffin already made for me. Yes, sir, I voted it and don't pretend to deny it before nobody. When I was going to the polls there was a man standing in the door and says, "Here comes you, God damn your soul. I have a coffin already made for you." I had two tickets in my pocket then; a Democratic ticket and a radial ticket; I pulled out the Democratic ticket and showed it to him, and he says, 'You are all right, go on.'*[45]

Thirteen years later, on February 18, 1884, Mrs. Violet Keeling was interviewed. The following is just a portion of that interview:

Question: *Are any of the colored people in your county Democrats?*

Answer: *I don't know. I don't have nothing to do with that sort.*

Question: *I ask you if any of them are Democrats?*

Answer: *I am telling you just what I know; I don't have nothing to do with that sort.*

Question: *Why do you have such a dislike to a colored man that votes the Democratic ticket?*

Answer: *I will tell you as near as I know. I think that if the race of colored people that has got no friends no how, and if they don't hang together they won't have none while one party is going one way and another the other. I don't wish to see a colored man sell himself when he can do without. Of course, we all have to live, and I always like to have a man live even if he works for 25 cents a day, but I don't want to see him sell himself away.*

Question: *Cannot a colored man vote the Democratic ticket without selling himself?*

Answer: *I think if a colored man votes the Democratic ticket he has already sold himself, because the white man is no friend to him anyway.*

Question: *Suppose your husband should go and vote a Democratic ticket?*

Answer: *I would just pick up my clothes and go to my father's, if I had a father, or would go to work for 25 cents a day.*[46]

What triggered the Senate investigations were letters to Congress from blacks in several Southern states. In those letters, black citizens reported a multitude of acts of terror. On March 25, 1871, a group of blacks from Kentucky sent a petition to Congress and stated the following:

Blacks From Kentucky

"We believe you are not familiar with the description of the Ku Klux Klan riding nightly over the country going from county to county and in the county towns spreading terror wherever they go, by robbing, whipping, ravishing, and killing our people without provocation, compelling Colored people to break ice and bathe in the chilly waters of the Kentucky River.

The Legislature has adjourned. They refused to enact any laws to suppress Ku Klux disorder. We regard them as now being licensed to continue their dark and bloody deeds under the cover of the dark night. They refuse to allow us to testify in the state courts where a white man is concerned. We find their deeds are perpetrated only upon Colored men and white Republicans. The Democratic Party has here a political organization composed only of Democrats - not a single Republican can join them.... We pray

that you will take some steps to remedy these evils listed below"
[in their home state of Kentucky].

December 24, 1867	A Colored schoolhouse was burned by incendiaries in Breckinridge.
January 28, 1868	Jim Macklin was taken from jail in Frankfort and hung.
May 28, 1868	Sam Davie was hung by a mob in Harrodsburg.
July 11, 1868	George Rogers was hung by a mob in Bradsfordsville, Martin County.
July 12, 1868	William Pierce was hung by a mob in Christian.
July 31, 1868	A Colored school exhibition was attacked by a mob in Midway.
August 3, 1868	Cabe Fields was shot and killed by disguised men near Keen Jessamine County.
August 7, 1868	Seven persons were ordered to leave their homes in Standford
August 1868	Silas Woodford, age sixty, was badly beaten by disguised mob. Also beaten were Mary Smith Curtis and Margret Mosby, near Keen Jessamine County.
August 1868	James Gaines was expelled from Anderson by Ku Klux Klan.
August 1868	James Parker was killed by the Klan in Pulaski County.
August 1868	Noah Blankenship was whipped by a mob in Pulaski County.
August 1868	William Gibson and John Gibson were hung by mob in Washington County.
August 21, 1868	Negroes were attacked, robbed, and driven from Summerville.
August 28, 1868	F.H. Montford was hung by a mob near Cogers Landing in Jessamine County.

September 1868	A Negro was hung by a mob.
September 1868	A U.S. Marshall named Meriwether was attacked, captured, and beaten to death by a mob in Larue County.
September 5, 1868	William Glassgow was killed by a mob in Warren County.
September 11, 1868	Two Negroes were beaten by the Klan in Anderson County.
September 11, 1868	Oliver Stone's house was attacked by mob in Fayette County.
September 18, 1868	A mob attacked Cumins' house and killed his daughter and a man named Adam in Pulaski County.
September 28, 1868	A mob killed Crasban Richardson at his home in Conishville.
October 26, 1868	A mob hung Terry Laws and James Ryan at Nicholasville.
December 1868	Two Negroes were shot by the Klan at Sulphur Springs in Union County.
December 1868	A Negro was shot at Morganfield Union County.
January 20, 1869	The Klan whipped William Parker in Lincoln County.
January 20, 1869	Albert Bradford was killed by men in disguise in Scott County.
March 12, 1869	The Klan whipped a boy at Stanford.
March 1869	Mr. Roberts was killed at the home of Frank Bournes in Jessamine County.
March 30, 1869	A mob hung George Bratcher on Sugar Creek in Garrard County.
May 29, 1869	A mob hung John Penny at Nevada Mercer County.
June 1869	The Klan whipped Lucien Green.
July 1869	A mob attacked Mr. Ronsey's home and killed three men and one woman.

July 2, 1869	The Klan whipped Mr. Miller.
July 1869	A mob killed Mr. & Mrs. Chas. Henderson on Silver Creek in Madison County.
July 17, 1869	A mob hung George Molling.
August 9, 1869	A mob hung James Crowders near Lebanon County.
August 1869	A mob tarred and feathered a citizen in Harrison County.
September 1869	The Klan burned down a Colored meeting house in Carol County.
September 1869	The Klan whipped a Negro at John Carmin's farm in Fayette County.
September 1869	A mob raided a Negro cabin and killed John Mosteran, Mr. Cash, and Mr. Coffey.
October 1869	The Klan killed George Rose in Madison County.[47]

(See Appendix C for a list of more terror)

Letters came from other states as well, including the following from Alabama.

(Portions of) Petition to President of the United States and
to U.S. Congress
From Blacks of Alabama in 1874

"...As a race, and as citizens, we never have enjoyed, except partially, imperfectly, and locally, our political and civil rights in this State. Our right to vote in elections has been, in a large portion of this state, denied, abridged, and rendered difficult and dangerous ever since we became voters. The means used by our political opponents to destroy or impair our right have been various, but chiefly consisted of violence in the form of secret assassinations, lynching, intimidation,

malicious and frivolous prosecutions, and arrest. And by depriving or threatening to deprive us of employment and renting of lands, which many of us, in our poverty and distress, were unable to disregard. These acts of lawlessness have been repeated and continued since our first vote in 1868, and their effect has been such that from 10 to 15,000 of the votes of our race have in each election been either repressed or been given under compulsion to our political opponents.

*A secret, powerful, vindictive, and dangerous organization composed exclusively of white men belonging to the **Democratic Party** in this state, and whose objects were to control the labor and repress or control the votes of the Colored citizens of this state. That organization, or a substitute and successor to it, under a changed name and a somewhat changed wardrobe and personal manifestation, still exists in all its hideous and fearful proportions. This organization we solemnly believe pervades all of the late rebellious States, and contains more than 100,000 arm-bearing men, most of whom are experienced and skilled in war. The definite political object of this organization is, by terror and violence, to make the citizenship and franchise of the Colored race, as established by the Constitution of the United States, practically and substantially a nullity.... "*[48]

Professor James McPherson reported that in 1872, when President Grant sent federal troops to install William P. Kellogg as governor of the State of Louisiana: *"Louisiana Democrats were infuriated. They formed White Leagues, which attacked black and white Republicans and took scores of lives. In one bloody affray at Colfax in April of 1873, 59 blacks were killed."*[49]

Thirty-six years after the Proclamation was signed, the May 4, 1899, edition of *New York Tribune* published the concerns of the National Afro-American Council of the United States. Herbert Aptheker records the following in his *Documentary History of Negro People.*

"The National Afro-American Council of the United States has issued a proclamation calling upon the colored people of this country to set apart Friday, June 2nd, as a day of fasting and prayer, and has called upon all colored ministers to devote the sunrise hour of the following Sunday, June 4th, to special exercises in order that God, the Father of Mercies, may take our deplorable case in His own hands, and that if vengeance is to be meted out, let God Himself repay.

"We are dragged before the courts by the thousands and sentenced to every form of punishment, and even executed, without the privilege of having a jury composed in whole or part of members of our own race, while simple justice should guarantee us judges and juries who could adjudicate our case free from the bias, caste, and prejudice incident to the same in this country.

In many sections we are arrested and lodged in jails on the most frivolous suspicion of being perpetrators of the most hideous and revolting crimes, and, regardless of established guilt, mobs are formed of ignorant, vicious, whiskey-besotted men, at whose approach the keys of these jails and prisons are surrendered and the suspicioned party is ruthlessly forced from the custody of the law and tortured, hung, shot, butchered, dismembered, and burned in the most fiendish manner. These mobs no longer conceal themselves in the shadows of the night, but in open day plunder the prisons for the victims of their lawless vengeance and defiantly walk into courts and rob the sheriffs and judges of their prisoners and butcher them without even time to commune in prayer with God, a privilege that no barbaric age has ever denied a soul about to be ushered into the presence of his Maker."[50] See Appendix B for a list of blacks who were lynched in the Southern states during 1900. Of the 100 lynchings that took place in 1900, ninety-four took place in Southern states, six took place in Northern states.

The terrorist attacks by the Democrats and their terrorist supporters were so horrendous, many believe that from the 1800s to the early 1900s this political party killed more people and destroyed more lives than the terrorist attacks attributed to Osama Bin Laden, the Al Qaeda, and the modern day Taliban of Afghanistan.

The Southern Democrats did everything in their power, using both lethal and legislative tactics to make African Americans second-class citizens or to completely deny them their rights as citizen. Northern Democrats, of course engaged in similar practices. According to Juan Williams, author of *Thurgood Marshall, American Revolutionary*, the Northern Democrats were involved in a variety of racist activities particularly in Baltimore Maryland in the late 1800s.

College Students Learn Democrats
Pass Laws to Isolate Blacks

In 1875, the Southern state of Tennessee adopted the first Jim Crow law. The law mandated that blacks be confined to separate sections of trains, depots, and wharves. Many states expanded the use of such laws to include many other facilities as well, including separate restrooms, drinking fountains, public parks and even cemeteries. Fifteen years later, in 1890, blacks were banned from white barbershops, hotels, restaurants, and theaters. By 1915, some Southern courts required black and white witnesses to swear on separate Bibles, and Oklahoma mandated separate telephone booths. Most of the schools were already segregated in both the North and South.

To stop the segregated practice that required separate railway carriages for whites and blacks, Homer Plessy filed a lawsuit against Judge John Ferguson of Louisiana in 1896 (*Plessy Vs Ferguson*). In response to the lawsuit, the U.S. Supreme Court handed down a landmark decision stating that it was legal to have separate facilities for blacks and whites, provided that the facilities were *equal*. The "Separate but Equal Doctrine" merely endorsed the racist practices that were sponsored and promoted by members of the Democratic Party.

Because the Jim Crow laws were established while the Republicans occupied the White House, Abolitionists and Radical Republicans were outraged with the Republican administration. Many moved down South in an attempt to bring about a change from within the Southern states, while others moved to the South to take advantage of "business opportunities" and who became known as "carpetbaggers." It was a struggle. The Democratic Party, along with their Klan supporters, were too powerful to overcome. Professor John Hope Franklin said, *"With the new franchise laws, with careful administration by white registrars who knew what they were doing, and with effective exclusion of Blacks from Democratic primaries, white supremacy in the realm of politics seemed to be permanently established."*[51] See Appendix I

Some of the Southern (separatist) practices were picked up by border Northern states, including states like Kansas. Prior to the Civil War, Kansas was one of the first states that was given the option of deciding whether or not it would be a "free state" or a "slave state." It was an important state for the Democrats and their pro-slavery supporters. The struggle between the Democrats and the Republicans to gain control of Kansas resulted in the death of many citizens in the small town of Lawrence, Kansas. In 1856, pro-slavery forces invaded Lawrence, burned several buildings and killed a number of citizens. After the massacre, Kansas was referred to as "Bleeding Kansas."

In 1954, ninety-eight years later, "Bleeding Kansas" became the battleground for another major battle. This battle was fought in the courts, not in the streets. The case, *Brown Vs the Board of Education of Topeka, Kansas*, was a landmark case testing *"the separate but equal doctrine"* practiced by the Topeka public schools. Fifty-eight years after the *Plessy Vs Ferguson* decision, the U.S. Supreme Court ruled that "the separate but equal doctrine" violated the Fourteenth Amendment and that *"it deprived children of equal education"* and was therefore *"unconstitutional."* The Fourteenth

Amendment was passed by a Republican administration 86 years earlier, in 1868. The court's landmark decision was the first step toward ending all forms of segregation; however the roots of racism ran deep, too deep to be uprooted by one landmark decision. Many thought that *Plessy Vs Ferguson* and *Brown Vs the Board of Education* would put an end to the Democrats' racist practices, but when the courts adjourned, the end was no where in sight.

Democrats have argued that all of these practices were established while the Republicans occupied the White House. The Republicans responded, "*Yes, this is true. But these racist practices were established under state law, not under federal law.*" Republicans argued that the federal government had no power to interfere with a state's right to pass their own laws unless those laws violated the Constitution. The Republicans also pointed out that it was their Fourteenth Amendment that brought about the landmark decision of *Brown Vs the Board of Education,* a decision that was not popular among the Democrats.

1960s: Blacks Give Democrats Their Vote
But Democrats Offer No Apology

It took many years, but change did come. The Civil Rights era of the late fifties and sixties was a time when more blacks became registered voters and more Democrats saw these new registered voters as their pathway to the White House. According to Historian, John Hope Franklin, the Democrats' new attitude (in the thirties and the sixties) regarding the African American vote was a complete reversal of how they used to think of them as voters. In his book, *Black Americans,* in referring to the period prior to the 1930s, Franklin said, "*The prevailing view of most Democrats was summed up by Mississippi's white senator, James K. Vardaman, who said: 'I am just as opposed to the Negro educator, Booker T. Washington, as a voter, with all his Anglo-Saxon reenforcements, as I am to the*

coconut-headed, chocolate-colored, typical little coon, Andy Dotson,
who blacks my shoes every morning.'"[52]

While the Republicans once again took our votes for granted,
the Democrats took the opportunity to get blacks to focus on their
immediate needs, rather than the past sins of the Democratic Party.
After the Roosevelt/Truman era, the Kennedys and other powerful
Democrats met with black leaders and convinced them that the
Republicans' past civil rights legislation didn't go far enough. They
told our leaders that they, the Democrats, were the party for African Americans, so like the Negroes of the thirties we gave them
our votes. They received our votes without ever apologizing for
the residual damage that resulted from their efforts to expand slavery and destroy Reconstruction, and without acknowledging that
they were the party that legislated many of the laws that caused us
great harm.

The Preacher and Politics

By 1961, America had a new president and the African Americans had a new party. With the party came programs, and with the
programs came the problems. Little did we realize that when we
gave the Democratic Party our votes, we also gave them the right
to be our political representatives, so whatever they supported, we
were politically obligated to support it as well. Why? Because
they now (supposedly) represented our beliefs, our values, our hopes
and dreams, and our best interests.

Prior to this time, the black clergy preached against many things
that the Democrats were supporting, issues such as:

1. The use of condoms and birth control for the sexually
   active teens and unmarried adults
2. Sex education in public schools
3. Abortions to solve unwanted pregnancies

    4. The elimination of prayer in schools and at graduation
       ceremonies
    5. Homosexual lifestyles

(Note: Black preachers never preached against the *person*, but against
the *acts* of homosexuality, adultery, and sex outside of marriage).

    These issues forced many African Americans to choose
between what they felt were God's laws and standards versus the
laws and standards adopted by their new political party. Some
felt they were caught between a rock and a hard place. Others
felt that if they rejected certain Democratic policies that conflicted
with their faith, black politicians would lose party support and
would be voted out of office during the next election. Some feared
that we would lose government programs that many felt we
needed. This schism between faith and politics remains a challenge even today.

    African Americans weren't the first group that had to make
the hard choice and choose between God and government. Blacks
knew from Scripture that Daniel and the Hebrew boys were faced
with this same predicament. The Babylonian government that
brought them from their homeland to be slaves offered them government positions and status in exchange for their loyalty. But they
refused and chose God over government.

    The question for many was *"Do we choose God's promises of
prosperity through obedience to His word or do we choose the
government's programs and compromise our Christian values?"*
This issue divided as many churches as the issue of slavery did for
white churches during the 1850s. In 1858, the issue of slavery
divided many denominations. During a speech on October 15, 1858,
Lincoln expressed his views regarding the white churches' split
over the issue of slavery. Lincoln said:

    *"Parties themselves may be divided and quarrel on minor
questions, yet it* [the debate regarding slavery] *extends beyond*

parties themselves. But does not this question make a distur-
bance outside the political circles? Does it not enter into the
churches and rend them asunder? What divided the great
Methodist Church into two parts, North and South? What has
raised this constant disturbance in every Presbyterian Gen-
eral Assembly that meets? What disturbed the Unitarian
Church in this very city two years ago? Is it not this same
mighty, deep-seated power that somehow operates on the minds
of men, exciting them and stirring them up in every avenue of
society—in politics, in religion, in literature, in morals in all
the manifold relations of life? Is this the work of politicians?
Is it that irresistible power which for fifty years has shaken
government and agitated the people to be stilled and subdued
by pretending that it is an exceedingly simple thing, and we
ought not to talk about it? "[53]

In the sixties, seventies, and eighties, churches no longer had
to deal with the issue of slavery; instead they were faced with
issues pertaining to abortions, homosexuality, sex education, and
prayer in school—and everyone felt a need to talk about it. These
issues took center stage as the new civil rights issues of the eighties, and like the churches of 1858, these issues caused division in
the same denominations that split over slavery one hundred years
earlier. Many churches took on these issues—while others sat quietly by in an effort to be politically correct. But as they sat, the
civil rights of African Americans were placed on the back burner,
and our communities started to deteriorate. Too few leaders wanted
to acknowledge this reality. Many sat in silence and watched the
moral decay take its toll on our people and on our communities.

Chapter Five

The Emperor Has No Clothes

Politicians were in denial, our people were in denial, and many of our religious leaders were in denial. No one wanted to acknowledge that the government's programs, no matter how well-intended, could not stop the moral, spiritual, and economic decay in the black community. Little did they realize that the politicians and our influential leaders, whether intentionally or unintentionally, were sacrificing our valucs and traditions for party loyalty.

It seemed as if the Democratic Party—the party that supposedly represented African Americans—could do no wrong. No one wanted to rock the boat. Few black leaders challenged their party, nor did many publicly acknowledge that the deplorable conditions in America's black communities were getting worse. Instead, at White House functions they grinned and smiled as if nothing was wrong. The only time our black leaders frowned was during the impeachment of President Clinton. Little did they realize that an impeachment process was taking place in our own black communities: Our traditional ways of living were being impeached by political apathy.

The situation reminded many of the children's story, *The Emperor's New Clothes*. The story tells of an Emperor who was so concerned with political popularity and public acceptance that he would do anything to get attention. One day he decided to have a new outfit made, which he would show off during a parade. The tailor who was selected to make the outfit had issues with Emperor

and seized the opportunity to embarrass him. He worked for weeks
and pretended to weave an outfit that really didn't exist. With a
keen sense of persuasion, he finally convinced the Emperor to try
on the "outfit." The naked Emperor convinced himself that it was
the most beautiful outfit he had ever seen and ordered his subjects
to prepare for the parade.

Everyone in town knew the purpose of the parade and was
anxious to see the Emperor's new clothes. As he paraded down
Main Street, stark naked, everyone admired the new outfit and saw
the Emperor as he wanted to be seen, not the way he really was—
naked, fat, flabby, and ugly. Finally a little boy yelled, *"The
Emperor has no clothes*!" He alone saw things as they really were,
spoke out, and told the unpopular naked truth. What he saw was
not beautiful—it was ugly, unattractive, and unappealing. The little
boy was the only one who was bold enough to tell the unpopular
"naked" truth.

The Naked Truth

What is the unpopular naked truth today? The truth is, our
communities are in decay and our people are in desperate need of
help. As stated in an earlier chapter:

a.   Our children are failing in school
b.   Our high school drop-out rate is still too high
c.   Our black-on-black crime is intolerable
d.   Our health conditions, such as high blood pressure, AIDS,
     diabetes, heart conditions, drug addiction, alcoholism,
     and sickle cell are all taking their toll on our people
e.   Many of our people have no health insurance
f.   Black gangs are creating terror in our neighborhoods
g.   Discrimination is still keeping many blacks out of well-
     paying jobs and from promotional opportunities

h. The dwindling number of two-parent households in the black community is a critical problem. (In 1940, 90 percent of the black households had two parents. In 1992 it had dropped to 30.5 percent)

i. Drugs, drug addiction, and the crimes associated with them are a major problem

j. Some of our music continues to degrade black women and black men

k. Our teenage girls and single women are having babies out of wedlock

l. Our churches appear to be more interested in their Sunday morning worship service than their Monday morning service to their community

m. Our political solutions are ineffective

Many of the problems that politicians claimed they had solutions for are the same problems that plagued the inner city of Washington, D.C., our nation's capitol. Just a stone's throw away from the White House, the United States Supreme Court, and the U.S. Congress, this city's conditions were so deplorable that inner-city children were preparing to die, rather than preparing to live. On November 1, 1993, the city's top newspaper, *The Washington Post*, featured the following front-page story: *"Getting ready to die young: Children in violent D.C. neighborhoods plan their own funerals."* DeNeen L. Brown, staff reporter for the *Post*, said:

"According to interviews with about 35 youth and adults who work with them, children as young as 10 have told friends how they want to be buried, what they want to wear and what songs they want played at their funeral. Community activists, social workers and psychologists who have studied the effects on young people living amid violence say children who plan their own funerals are showing that they do not expect to live long. According to the D.C. Department of Human Services, 50.8 percent of young people 15-24 years old who died in the

*city during the last decade were victims of homicide. William
W. Johnson, a former police officer who works with the youth
in the District, said death is almost a daily reality for some.* "[54]

There was no national response from either the White House
or the Congressional Black Caucus when this story was released.
However, shortly after, when a young white girl named Polly Klaas
was kidnapped and killed, President Clinton held a press conference and specifically spoke against that killing. His statement
seemed to suggest that the death of one twelve-year-old white girl
in Los Angeles was far more important than the number of young
black children who are killed each week in Washington, D.C. In
1955, when a fourteen-year-old black teenager from Chicago named
Emmett Till was abducted, severely beaten, and thrown into the
river with a weight fastened around his neck with barbed wire, it
made national news. Today, it is no longer news when a black
child dies. It is considered to be the norm, not the exception.

The Naked Truth About the Clinton Administration

The fact that Clinton had nothing to say regarding the death of
the young black children in D.C. made it easier to understand why
black Secret Service agents felt his administration was insensitive to
their needs and filed a discrimination lawsuit against that administration. It also helps us to understand why so many African Americans are fired from their jobs by the federal government. On December
14, 1993, the *Knight Ridder Newspaper* released an article by
reporter, Frank Greves, entitled: *"Most Federal Firings Are Minority."* Greves opens his featured story with the following statement:

*"The federal government, America's biggest employer and
supposedly one of its most colorblind, fired minority workers
at more than twice the rate of whites last year. Minority men
were dismissed at more than three times the rate of all whites,
and minority women at double the rate of whites."* [55]

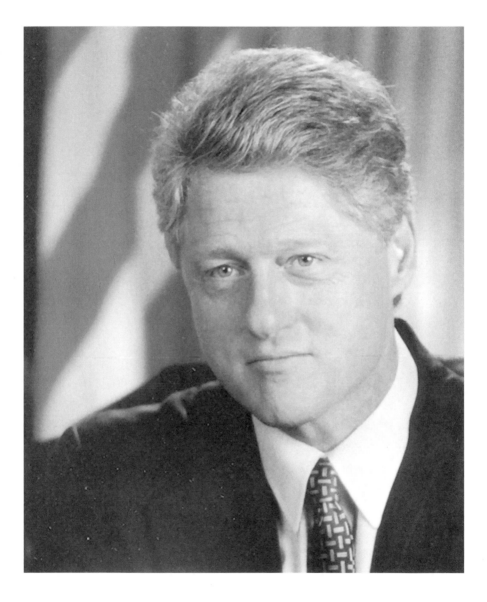

President Bill Clinton
What specifically did he do for African Americans?

In addition to this shocking news, the Equal Employment Opportunity Commission reported that it administratively closes over 90 percent of all racial discrimination complaints without ever investigating them. The naked truth is this: If minorities can't trust the federal government to process their discrimination complaints, or trust it to retain minorities as employees, who can they trust to enforce the civil rights laws?

During the eight years of his presidency, Clinton and the Democrats promised much, but produced very little beyond lip service. They seemed to do just enough to get the black vote, but no more. No one expected that during the Clinton administration Democrat-controlled states and major colleges would start dismantling Affirmative Action Programs or start voting against them. Clinton and the Democrats promised to protect and preserve these types of programs, not stand by and watch them disappear.

When the question is asked—*"What specifically did the Clinton administration do for African Americans?"*—Most respond by citing the significant number of African Americans that he appointed to various offices during his administration. But appointees are meaningless if they fail to respond to the cries of their people or if they are not listened to by the administration. We will address their failure to respond to the cries of our people later on in the chapter. But first, let us review a situation where Clinton ignored the advice of one of his black appointees, and how his lack of respect for her counsel resulted in the death of several hundred thousand Africans.

Clinton appointed Prudence Bushnell to the position of Deputy Secretary over African Affairs within the State Department. As early as April 6, 1994, Secretary Bushnell warned the Clinton administration that the killing of Rwanda's president would probably produce widespread violence, and that the country's military had plans to temporarily take control of the country, but Clinton took no action. While Clinton continued to ignored this black woman's counsel and warnings, during the following sixty days, an estimated 800,000 Africans were massacred. When Clinton visited Rwanda

four years later, in March of 1998, he expressed deep
remorse for his administration's apathy. But when it came to Bosnia,
he did not have to express remorse. He sent 20,000 troops to stop
the bloodshed in Europe's Bosnia, but he turned a deaf ear to the
warning that would have stopped the massacre in Africa's Rwanda.

Those who boast about Clinton's appointments should be asked
the following questions: How did President Clinton's appointees
affect, address, or remedy the specific problems facing African
Americans?   Did the appointees and the Clinton administration
solve, resolve, or address the specific problems facing African
Americans? As a race, are African Americans better off today than
they were before President Clinton took office?

Ebony Magazine didn't seem to think so. During the Presidential Campaign of 2000, *Ebony's* reporter asked Vice President
Al Gore and Governor George Bush a series of questions pertaining to issues affecting African Americans. The questions seem to
imply that these needs and issues still existed or had not been properly addressed during Clinton's years in office. The following are
a sample of the questions asked in *Ebony's* November 2000 issue:

1. *Even in this time of unparalleled domestic prosperity,
   we see signs of a widening economic gap between blacks
   and whites. Blacks have not, by and large, benefited
   from the recent economic growth. And while unemployment, even among historically underemployed black
   teens has decreased, we still find too many African
   Americans in low-paying, low-skilled jobs. If elected,
   what would you do to close the economic gap to help
   African Americans gain a better foothold in the booming high-tech economy?*

2. *Fair-minded individuals of both parties say we still have
   not created a level playing field for minorities to compete equally for employment, business, and educational*

opportunities—yet affirmative action programs are under increased attack, and several of our largest states have abolished programs designed to address historic inequities that have thwarted minority progress. In light of this, how you would create educational and economic opportunities for minorities?

3. *Racial profiling—the practice of targeting and harassing innocent blacks as crime suspects—has gained attention as a national problem. How can we as a nation put a stop to this form of discrimination?*

4. *The schools of our inner cities face major challenges, including outmoded facilities, an aging teaching corps, and social and crime problems that accompany children to school each day, making learning difficult. Given the accelerated pace of education in more affluent school districts, what would you do as president to keep our cities from falling further behind academically and, as a result, economically?*

5. *A recent study by the Human Rights Watch indicates that, although drug use among whites is five times greater, blacks in states like Illinois are incarcerated 57 times more often than whites for drug-related offenses. If elected, what would you do about these and other documented disparities in the arrest and sentencing of blacks and whites, not only for drug possession and sale, but also for other offenses?"*[56]

Neither candidate answered any of the questions directly or satisfactorily, but what was most disturbing was the fact that Vice President Gore never cited one thing that the Clinton administration did during the previous eight years to address any of the inequities. In contrast, during other interviews when the Vice

President was asked about the economy, foreign affairs, and the number of African Americans the Clinton administration appointed to top positions, Gore proudly boasted about these accomplishments. There was no such boasting when asked about blacks in low-paying jobs and poor schools, or the problems concerning crime and racial discrimination.

When *Ebony* asked about reparation pay to compensate African Americans for the *"lingering effects of slavery,"* Vice President Gore said: *"The best reparation is good education and affirmative action."* He never addressed the compensation issue nor did he acknowledge the significant role that the Democrats played in keeping slavery alive or his party's efforts to disenfranchise African Americans and make them second-class citizens after the passage of the Emancipation Proclamation – a period lasting from Reconstruction to the late 1950s. President Clinton and most white Democrats say little regarding supporting blacks in their quest for reparation pay, even though they claim to be the friends of blacks.

In May 2001, *Savoy* magazine published an article written by Jill Nelson entitled "We've been Bill-boozled." In the article Nelson said, *"For eight years we have embraced Bill Clinton as an honorary soul brother. The puzzling thing is, we looked the other way as he hung us out to dry. We shout that we love him and cheer as if he's actually done something for us besides, as James Brown puts it, talking loud and saying nothing."*[57] Nelson also condemned President Clinton for giving Carlos Vignali a presidential pardon after he was convicted of *"importing 800 pounds of cocaine into the inner city of Minneapolis,"* but did not offer pardons to African American candidates who were more deserving of such pardons.

On December 3, 2002, two years after Clinton left the White House, C-Span (Cable TV) aired Bill Clinton's speech to the Democratic Leadership Council at New York State University. The speech dealt with several important issues that he felt the Democratic Party should focus on if they wanted to regain the White House and control of the Senate. None of the issues that he discussed pertained to civil rights for African Americans. His only reference to civil rights pertained to civil rights for gays—he made no references to improving the conditions of African Americans. In fact, there were no references to African Americans or to the conditions of their communities. However, he did stress that America needed to revisit the Marshall Plan to rebuild communities in other countries. His last comments were: *"People will have more respect for a leader who is strong and wrong, than for a leader who is weak and right."*

Clinton wasn't the only Democratic president that was weak on civil rights. Dr. King had problems with the Kennedy administration as well. Contrary to what many African Americans may believe, Dr. King was not a diehard Democrat who looked the other way when the Democrats failed to keep their promises on civil rights issues. King didn't hide their failures; he exposed their failures. In his book *Why We Can't Wait*, King said the following about the Kennedy administration: *"The feeling was growing among Negroes that the administration had oversimplified and underestimated the civil rights issue. President Kennedy, if not backing down, had backed away from a key pledge of his campaign – to wipe out housing discrimination immediately with a stroke of the pen. When he had finally signed the housing order, two years after taking office, its terms, though praiseworthy, had revealed a serious weakness in its failure to attack the key problem of discrimination in financing by banks and other institutions.*

"While Negroes were being appointed to some significant jobs and social hospitality was being extended at the White House to Negro leaders, the dreams of the masses remained in tatters. The Negro felt that he recognized the same old bone that had been tossed to him in the past – only now it was being handed to him on a platter, with courtesy.

"With each new Negro protest, we were advised, sometimes privately and sometimes in public, to call off our efforts and channel all of our energies into registering voters. On each occasion we would agree with the importance of voting rights, but would patiently seek to explain that Negroes did not want to neglect all other rights while one was selected for concentrated attention.

"Kennedy's administration appeared to believe it was doing as much as politically possible and had, by its positive deeds, earned enough credit to coast on civil rights."[58] See Appendix H 1964 Civil Rights Act

Unlike the black leadership of today, Dr. King was more committed to solving the problems of the people, rather than being socially accepted by political parties that ignored the concerns of his people. Because many modern-day black leaders seem to be more interested in being invited to White House functions, rather than finding social solutions to help their communities function, they remained silent when they should have spoken out to expose Clinton's failures and apathy. As Dr. King so noted, *"While social hospitality was being extended at the White House to Negro leaders, the dreams of the masses remained in tatters."* In other words, it didn't take much to buy the silence of some of our black leaders both during the Kennedy era and the Clinton era. Silence for many was purchased with a simple White House dinner invitation.

Future Loyalty To Democratic Party

Will African Americans remain loyal to the Democratic Party? According to the *1989 Fifth Edition of the Negro Almanac*, the answer is no, particularly for those thirty and under. The Almanac reports that surveys by the Joint Center for Political Studies reveal that blacks under thirty tend to identify with the Republicans. Experts say the reasons for this can be attributed to the under thirties' remoteness to the civil rights struggle and their feelings that issues like civil rights are no longer the subject of intense political focus. The Almanac reports that many blacks have placed at the top of their agenda, *"issues of national and individual economic well being in an increasingly competitive and complex global economy. As segments of this population increase and as they move further away from the tumultuous years of the Civil Rights Movement,"*[59] they become better acquainted with the roles that both parties played in their history. The *Negro Almanac* predicts, *"Blacks are likely to find it easier to support a progressive Republican Party."*

Chapter Six

Black Leadership Evaluation

Of all the truths, none are as difficult to accept as those associated with ineffective black leadership. However each year, more and more African Americans are openly expressing their displeasure with our current leaders and the organizations they represent.

Writing for *Savoy* Magazine, Deborah Mathis, a Shorenstein Fellow at Harvard University, said: *"The Congressional Black Caucus, which was founded in 1971 by 13 Black members of Congress, started out well. But by the 80s, the CBC was weary and worn, with virtually no legislative trophies to show for its scars. By many accounts, the body that was once a force to be reckoned with has not only lost its fervor but its political power as well. Critics say that the Caucus grew complacent under what was generally accepted as a friendly Clinton administration, and many wondered whether the CBC may be past its prime."* In reference to the Caucus's Annual Conference, which draws many famous people, including movie stars, Mathis said: *"Aside from the daily workshops, the weekend is such a feast of fashion, schmoozing, and carousing that it can never be said the CBC is good for nothing."*[60]

Criticism of our black leadership by black citizens and by other black leaders is not a new phenomenon. During the beginning of Dr. King's Civil Rights movement he told *Playboy* magazine that he talked to a crowd of two hundred black ministers and challenged them to do more than just preach about the glories of heaven to their people. He told them *"A minister cannot preach the glories of heaven while ignoring the social conditions in his own community that caused men an earthly hell."*

Just three years after the death of Rev. Dr. Martin Luther King Jr., actor Ossie Davis, addressed the 1971 Congressional Black Caucus Conference. On June 18, 1971, he told the audience to stop blaming the white man for their problems. He said, *"**It's not the man, it's the plan**. Blacks do not need a bunch of rhetoric* from their leaders. Blacks ***need a map***, not their leader's ***rap***. He challenged the Caucus to come up with Ten Black Commandments that would offer a simple, moral, intelligent plan that blacks could carry in their heart.[61] Thirty years later, the Caucus apparently is still working on the plan and the commandments because no one has seen either.

Most African Americans are aware of what the Caucus and the Clinton administration did for the gay community, but few to none can specifically state what they did to address the **specific** needs of Black Americans. Using the black experience as a springboard to launch their own agenda, gay rights groups obtained medical coverage for their live-in lovers, the right to adopt children, the right to marry in some states, and a *"don't ask, don't tell policy"* in the military. But no one can *tell* what the Congressional Black Caucus or our leaders (such as Jesse Jackson) did to address the pressing needs of African Americans.

Both Jackson and members of the Caucus showed their compassion and concern for the various gay rights groups, but that same compassion and concern has yet to reach the oppressed black community. Some blacks have said, *"If a black leader can travel overseas and successfully negotiate the freedom of American hostages, why can't he devote the same amount of time to free his own people who are hostages and victims of gang violence, drug addiction, and teenage pregnancies?"*

Samuel Cotton, author of *Silent Terror: An African American Journey Into Contemporary Slavery*, wasn't upset with Jesse Jackson because he traveled overseas to negotiate the freedom of American hostages. Cotton was upset because he felt our powerful black leaders have ignored those who are hostage to the black slave trade in Africa. Cotton accused Jackson, the Congressional Black Caucus, and other powerful black leaders of consistently ignoring the modern-day enslavement of Black Africans in Muslim-controlled African countries. As noted in an earlier chapter, the Muslim's historical connection with the African slave trade is well documented.

During the past decade, other blacks have also expressed their concerns about black leadership. In a nationwide poll conducted by Janice Hayes of *Detroit News* and Ellyn Ferguson of Gannett News Service, 1,211 blacks reported: *"Civil rights groups are falling behind the times and not keeping up with the problems facing blacks in the 1990s."* Their findings were highlighted in a front-page article released *by USA Today* on February 24, 1992, entitled: "Civil Rights Groups Out of Step." They reported that blacks wanted their leadership to *"fight crime, help the poor, and improve education."*[62]

Nine years later, on August 18, 2001, an international magazine called the *Economist* expressed similar feelings about today's civil rights leaders. The article entitled, "The Leadership of Black America: Time to Pass on the Torch" said: *"Rarely out of the headlines, masters of the stage-managed event and the attention-grabbing sound bite, men like Mr. Jackson and Mr. Sharpton have long used the power of publicity to prod white America into recognizing the claims of black America, and doing something to meet those claims. But, for all their past successes, their grandstanding now looks tired and increasingly irrelevant. To a growing number of blacks, their ideas have gone stale. The problems of America's blacks have changed considerable over the past four decades, but their leadership has not."*[63]

PBS Commentator Tony Brown said in his book *Black Lies, White Lies*: *"Black leadership in this country has scrupulously avoided having a plan of action or a road map to equality either because they are not smart enough (which I doubt is the case) or because they don't want blacks to leave the **Democratic plantation**. My concerns about the failure of America's black leadership* *are no different from those of many blacks, most of whom prefer to keep their feelings private because they are not politically correct among the black elite.*"[64]

Today's leaders could learn from black leaders of the past. Booker T. Washington, who was both a Republican and a very powerful black leader of his time, presented the following plan for the black community during his National Negro Conference in 1896:

1. *"We are more and more convinced, as we gather in these Annual Conferences, that we shall secure our rightful place as citizens in proportion as we possess **Christian character**, education, and property. To this end we urge parents to exercise rigid care in the control of their children, the doing away with the one-room cabin and the mortgage habit.*
2. *We urge the purchase of land, improved methods of farming, diversified crops, attention to stock raising, dairying, fruit growing, and more interest in learning the trades, now too much neglected.*
3. *We urge that a larger proportion of our college-educated men and women give the race the benefit of their education, along industrial lines, and that more educated ministers and teachers settle in the country districts.*
4. *As in most places, the public schools are in session only three or four months during the year, we urge the people by every means possible, to supplement this time by at least three or four additional months each year, that no sacrifice be considered too great to keep the children in school, and that only the best teachers be employed.*
5. *We note with pleasure, the organization of other Conferences, and we advise that the number be still more largely increased."*[65]

This was the type of plan that Ossie Davis and Tony Brown were referring to. So far, our black leaders have not come up with

Booker T. Washington
In addition to blacks developing vocational skills, he wanted
them to develop Christian character.

such a plan. Perhaps they are still looking for one of the two political parties to do the planning for them.

Black Leadership and Affirmative Action

In 1995, several African American, Hispanic, and female longshore workers from Seattle and Tacoma (Washington) became disenchanted with our black leadership when they attempted to sue their union and one hundred major shipping companies for racial and sexual discrimination. When they requested support from President Bill Clinton, the NAACP, Rev. Jesse Jackson, and the Congressional Black Caucus, only one member of the Caucus wrote a letter in support of them, Congressman Donald Payne. President Clinton, Rev. Jackson, Maxine Waters, and the NAACP all turned a deaf ear to their cries and chose not to respond to their phone calls and letters. Alexis Herman, President Clinton's newly appointed African American Secretary of Labor, also ignored their cry for help. One man asked: *"What good are African American politicians and appointees if they turn their backs on their people? If a white person had these same positions and they turned their backs on blacks, we would call them racist. But what do we call blacks who turn their backs on their own people?"*

Ironically, the longshore workers' discrimination lawsuits were filed shortly after the Clinton administration filed a reverse discrimination suit against Illinois State University on behalf of a group of *white janitors* in 1995. Without the support of our black leaders or the President's black appointees, the longshore workers won their cases after several workers came forward and testified on behalf of the African Americans, Hispanics, and female workers.

White workers verified the plaintiffs' claims that the word *"Nigger"* was often used in the workplace. In fact, shipping companies in Tacoma, Washington, had a job classification called *"Nigger Jobs."* One worker testified that she was present when an African American longshoreman fell off the ship into water amongst a log boom, and as he struggled for his life, white workers shouted, "***Drown, Nigger, Drown.***" She said no one would help him, including management. Other workers told the court that women were threatened, called offensive names, and some were nearly raped. Hispanics testified of their experiences as well.

All of this information along with a multitude of other documentation including a four-page featured news article by *The Seattle Times* was given to the Clinton administration and to our black leadership, but they still turned a deaf ear to the workers' plea for justice. Again, all three groups won their case without the support of our key black leaders and the Clinton administration. Years ago, blacks knew who they could depend on. Today, many blacks, like the longshore workers, are not sure.

Clinton Administration Ignore's Court Order

The story didn't end there. During the investigative stage of the lawsuit, the longshoremen learned that the Clinton administration had refused to comply with a 1994 court order that required that his Secretary of Labor force these same shipping companies to develop an Affirmative Action Plan. In the case of *Charles Fairchild Vs the Department of Labor and Secretary Robert Reich* (case #CV92-5765 Kn), Federal Judge David V. Kenyon issued an order to Robert Reich, Secretary of Labor, to force the shipping companies to produce a comprehensive Affirmative Action Plan within sixty days or explain to the court why it had not been done. This order was issued twelve months before the longshore workers filed their discrimination lawsuits. President Clinton left office without ever having his Secretary of Labor comply with the federal court's order, which stated:

"Undertake a prompt and reasonable investigation of the Pacific Maritime Association's [the shipping companies']

*compliance with the written Affirmative Action Plan require-
ments of 41 C.F.R. paragraphs 60-250.5 and 60-741.5. Within
60 days of the date of this order, and every 60 days thereafter
until the issue of PMA's (the Pacific Maritime Association)
compliance with the aforementioned written Affirmative
Action Plan requirements is resolved, to serve on the Plaintiffs [Longshoremen] and this court with a report indicating
the steps the Defendants [the Clinton administration] have
taken and the steps the Defendants are planning to take to
fulfill their enforcement responsibilities under Section 503.* "[66]

As of the beginning of 2003, the shipping companies have yet
to produced the court-ordered Affirmative Action Plan. Nor had
the Congressional Black Caucus ever applied any pressure to force
Clinton and/or his Secretary of Labor to comply with the order.

Affirmative Action: Who Supports It?

If you were to ask an African American which party supports
affirmative action and which one opposes it, the average person
will probably say the Democrats support it and the Republicans
oppose it. Many who believe this to be true often base their opinion on the fact that there are a number of Republicans who feel that
racial quotas are discriminatory. However, most people, including
some of the modern-day Republicans, are not aware of the fact that
affirmative action programs were actually launched by the Republicans, not the Democrats. The first programs were initiated shortly
after President Nixon appointed Arthur S. Fletcher, an African
American himself, as chairman of U.S. Civil Rights Commission
and signed into law the Equal Employment Opportunities Act of
1972. The Civil Rights Commission was first established in 1958
under another Republican president, Dwight D. Eisenhower.

Not all Republicans are against affirmative action programs.
Individuals such as J.C Watts, Steve Largent, Condoleezza Rice, and
Colin Powell still strongly support them. In a speech to the 2000

Republican National Convention, Powell said, *"We must understand the cynicism that exists in the black community, the kind of cynicism that is created when, for example, some in our party miss no opportunity to roundly and loudly condemn affirmative action that helped a few thousand black kids get an education, but you hardly heard a whimper from them over affirmative action for lobbyists who load our federal tax codes with preferences for special interests."* Many blacks and Democrats condemn President George W. Bush for calling the University of Michigan's (affirmative action) points program for minority students, "constitutionally flawed," but few condemned President Clinton's brief in support of the white janitor's reverse discrimination claim against Illinois State University. Nor did they condemn him (Clinton) for turning his back on black, Hispanic, and female longshore workers and for refusing to comply with a court order that required an affirmative action plan from the shipping companies.

Even though the facts show that some Republicans support it while others oppose it, the general feeling is that Republicans as a whole are against affimative action and Democrats as a whole are for it. However, when you consider the noncompliance on the part the Clinton administration in regards to Judge Kenyon's orders and the lack of response by the Congressional Black Caucus in the matter of the black longshoreman, their actions seem to imply that the Republicans are not the only ones who may have a problem with supporting affirmative action programs.

More Politicians - Fewer Problems?

One might think that having more black politicians would mean fewer black problems, but such has not proven to be the case. There were seventeen African American members of the House of Representatives in 1980. Thirteen years later in 1993, their numbers had risen to forty, but no major differences had occurred in the problems facing African Americans. In some areas, the conditions were slightly worse. Consider this: In 1980, with seventeen black members in the House of Representatives, 1,826,000 black families were living in poverty (28 percent) and 60.1 percent of blacks had private health insurance.

In 1993, when there were forty black members in House of Representatives, the number of black families living in poverty increased to 2,499,000 (31.3 percent), while the number of blacks with private health insurance decreased to 52 percent.[67]

Other evidence of a decline in the standard of living of African Americans was revealed in a study conducted by the University of Michigan. The study shows that, from 1994 to 1999, black family wealth declined despite a booming economy and an increased number of black politicians. According to the study, the net worth of the median black household fluctuated—half were higher and half were lower—decreasing from $8400 to $7500. The study went on to say that for every dollar of wealth, the median white household had in 1999, the median black household held barely 9 cents.

In the sixties, when we had fewer black politicians, we had lower unemployment. The chart in Appendix D shows the number of persons receiving unemployment compensation each year. The numbers do not reflect the actual percentage of all who are unemployed, only those receiving unemployment compensation. When a person is no longer receiving unemployment benefits they are classified as employed whether they have found a job or not. In 1965, when our unemployment was only 8.5 percent, we had fewer black politicians, but we also had the Rev. Dr. Martin Luther King Jr. In 1970, when our unemployment went down to 6.7 percent, Dr. King's residual presence was still a factor. In the mid-seventies, our unemployment reached double digits and has remained there every since. Unemployment increased during the same period when the number of black politicians increased.

This is not to suggest that black elected officials aren't needed nor is it to suggest that black elected officials are ineffective. It is to say that, as taxpayers, we must hold all politicians accountable, whether they are black or white, Republican or Democrat. Failure to do so will only prolong our pains and problems.

Many black religious leaders believe the pressing problems facing African Americans ***are not*** the results of ineffective black leadership alone, even though effective leadership can make a difference. They believe many of our problems stem from lifestyle choices—that is, choosing to walk away from God and His principles—rather than walking with God and using His principles to unite and change our community. Unfortunately, only a handful of our national leaders today are challenging our people to walk with God and accept responsibility for our own behavior.

Writing for the *Wall Street Journal*, reporter Jason Riley says: *"There was a time when black liberals, too, knew the difference between black responsibility and white oppression."* In 1961, Dr. King told a congregation, *"We know that there are many things wrong in the white world, but there are many things wrong in the black world too. We can't keep on blaming the white man. There are things we must do for ourselves. Do you know that Negroes are 10 percent of the population of St. Louis and responsible for 58 percent of its crime? We got to face that. And we got to do something about our moral standard."*[68]

Rev. Joseph E. Lowery of the Southern Christian Leadership Conference said if Dr. King were alive today, he would have as much to say to his people as he would to the politicians and corporate America. Rev. Lowery believes King would *"call for a liberation of lifestyles that would make us free at last, in this life. Free from confused priorities, free from dependency on drugs and alcohol. Free from abuse of sexuality, free to support black institutions and businesses. Free to support and love ourselves, and free to turn to each other and not on each other."* Rev. Benjamin L. Hooks said, *"Dr. King, a Southern preacher who earned his doctorate in theology, had a consistent message taken from the Scripture."*[69]

Rev. Hooks, Rev. Lowery, and the Rev. Dr. Martin Luther King Jr. all knew that when we, as a race, walked with God, we made forward progress with each godly step. They and other ministers believe that when we, as a race, walked away from God, our steps took us backward not forward. They believe that it was our faith in God, not our faith in government, that made a major and positive difference in our lives.

Former Congressman Floyd Flake of New York is a prime example of how a person's faith in God, rather than his or her political affiliation can change a community. Many believe that this ordained minister did more for his community as a pastor than he did as a Congressman. When this former member of the U.S. House of Representatives left Congress and went back to his community in Queens, New York, he developed expensive commercial and residential projects, private schools, and a variety of social commercial and social services enterprises. Pastor Flake and his Allen A.M.E. church of 10,000 members now have the unique distinction of being the largest African American employer in New York City. In his book, *The Way of The Bootstrapper*, Pastor Flake says, *"I believe that **without God, none of it would be possible.** "*[70] Rev. Flake is the true personification of what a modern-day black leader should be.

African American Accountability
Report Card for Leadership

It is important that we hold everyone accountable who claims that they are working on behalf of African Americans. On an annual basis, every politician and every national leader should be evaluated to determine what efforts, if any, were made on behalf of their African American constituents. Politicians are the employees of the people. If corporations can conduct annual Performance Appraisals to determine whether an employee has fulfilled his or her job requirements, the citizens who employ the politicians should feel obligated to do the same. If you could, how would you rate our leaders and politicians? Well, here is your opportunity to determine whether or not the specific needs of the African Americans

Congressman Floyd Flake
He is the personification of what a black leader should be.

were addressed during the Clinton era. On a **separate sheet
of paper**, answer the following questions truthfully:

Issue: Black-on-Black Crime

What specifically did the Clinton administration do to address
black-on-black crime? What laws were passed? What policies
were developed? What specific programs were started to address
these types of crimes? How successful were the laws, policies,
and programs?

What specifically has the Congressional Black Caucus done
to address black-on-black crime during the past eight years? What
laws did they introduce? What policies did they develop? What
programs did they start to specifically address these types of crimes?
How successful were their laws, policies, and programs?

What specifically did the NAACP, Urban League, and/or the
Rainbow Coalition do to address black-on-black crime during the
past eight years? What programs did they develop to specifically
address this issue? How successful were their programs?

Using the same wording in the questions above, evaluate the
Clinton administration, the Caucus, and the various African American organizations in each of the following areas listed below. State
specifically what each has done during the past decade to address
each of the following issues. Also state whether or not you
feel their programs, policies, and/or laws have been effective and/
or successful.

Evaluating Issues Affecting African Americans

What have the politicians and various organizations done to
address these issues:

Inner-city gang violence

African American teenage pregnancies
Drug sales in the black community
High school dropouts and low test scores
High unemployment among African American males
Racial profiling and racial bias in court decisions
Poverty among African Americans
Sickle cell research and its progress
Improvement of quality of inner city schools

The Accountability Report Card is not a tool to merely evaluate one party or one group. It is a process to hold accountable any person claiming to be working on our behalf. It matters not whether they are members of the Democratic Party or the Republican Party, or whether they are a part of an organization that represents black issues. Every person and organization must be evaluated. Without an evaluation system, there can be no way to measure the effectiveness of our leaders and our organizations.

Many of our politicians and organizations have done some of the right things for the wrong reasons. Many black citizens believe some of our leaders were motivated by their own selfish ambitions, and not by the pressing needs of the people. The same can be said about today's Democratic Party.

Chapter Seven

The Democrats' Racist Past

But No Formal Apology

During this fact-finding investigation, we reviewed the work of several historians, and none of our nation's leading history professors seem to give the Democrats high marks for their treatment of African Americans, particularly during the period of slavery and Reconstruction. Included among the materials reviewed were books by Professor James M. McPherson of Princeton University, Professor John Hope Franklin of Brooklyn College, Professor David Herbert Donald of Harvard, Professor Allen W. Trelease of the University of North Carolina, and Professor Howard O. Lindsey of DePaul University.

Historians say that after the Civil War, when Republicans passed various laws and developed a number of social programs, such as the Freedmen's Bureau, to assist blacks, the Democrats became very angry and resentful. From their deep-seated anger, several terrorist organizations were born; and in their efforts to gain the upper hand, the Democrats became the *"Daddy"* of the Ku Klux Klan. *The Encyclopaedia Britannica* reported that the *"Democrat's resentment led to the formation of the secret terroristic organizations such as the Ku Klux Klan and the Knights of the White Camelia. The use of fraud, violence, and intimidation helped Southern conservatives regain control of their state governments. By the time the last federal troops had been withdrawn in 1877, the Democratic Party was back in power."*[71] See Appendix H 1898-1940 and Appendix I.

Professor Allen Trelease, author *of Reconstruction: The Great Experience,* said: *"Klansmen in disguise rode through Negro neighborhoods at night warning Negroes either to cast **Democratic** ballots or stay away from the poll. The Klan also sent notices to Republican office holders, warning them of death and telling them to either resign or leave the vicinity. Similar notices went to active Republicans of both races and often to the teachers of Negro schools as well. Klan activities created a reign of **terror** in many localities and sometimes had the desired effect of demoralizing Negroes and Republicans.... **Republicans** of both races were threatened, beaten, shot, and murdered with impunity. In some areas Negroes stopped voting or voted the **Democrat** ticket as the Klan demanded."* Trelease went on to say, **"***Democrats, by a kind of tortured reasoning, sometimes accused Negroes and Republicans of attacking and even killing each other so that the crimes would be blamed on the Democrats; investigations usually revealed that the Democrats had committed the acts themselves."*[72]

Professors John Hope Franklin and Alfred Moss, authors of *From Slavery To Freedom,* tells us that, *"The Camelias and the Klan were the most powerful of the secret orders. Armed with guns, swords, or other weapons, their members patrolled some parts of the South day and night. They used intimidation, force, ostracism in business and society, bribery at the polls, arson, and even murder to accomplish their deed. Depriving the Negro of political equality became, to them, a holy crusade in which a noble end justified any means. Negroes were run out of communities if they disobeyed orders to desist from voting; and the more resolute and therefore insubordinate blacks were whipped, maimed, and hanged. In 1871 several Negro officials in South Carolina were given fifteen days to resign and they were warned that if they failed to do so, then retributive justice will as surely be used as night follows day. For many white Southerners, violence was still the surest means of keeping the Negroes politically impotent, and in countless communities they were not allowed, under penalties of reprisals, to show their faces in town on Election Day. It had looked as though the Civil War would break out anew as the Democrats resorted to every possible device to overthrow the radicals."*[73]

Professor Franklin went on to say from his book entitled *Reconstruction After the Civil War, "It was reported that in North Carolina the Klan was responsible for 260 outrages, including 7 murders and the whipping of 72 whites and 141 Negroes. In one county in South Carolina, 6 men were murdered and more than 300 were whipped during the first six months of 1870. The personal indignities inflicted upon individual whites and Negroes were so varied and so numerous as to defy classification or enumeration."*[74]

In his book, *The Abolitionist Legacy,* Professor James McPherson reported, *"In 1873, Louisiana became almost a synonym for chaos and violence. When Grant sent federal troops to install Kellogg in office* [as governor], *Louisiana Democrats were infuriated. They formed White Leagues which attacked black and white Republicans and took scores of lives."*[75]

From his book entitled *Charles Sumner,* Harvard Professor David Herbert Donald reached the following conclusion: *"Congress could give the Negro the vote, but all over the South the Ku Klux Klan and other terrorist organizations systematically intimidated the freedmen, flogged or slaughtered their leaders, and drove whites who worked with them into exile. Congress could require federal troops to supervise the registration of voters, but Negroes were waylaid and butchered on the roads to the registration offices. Congress could suppress outright violence by military force, but it could do nothing to protect Negroes from landlords who told them bluntly: If you vote with that Yankee* [Republican] *party, you shall not live on our land."*[76]

Professor Howard O. Lindsey, the author of *A History of Black Americans,* says, *"Blacks and sympathetic whites were attacked and threatened. African Americans were discouraged from seeking elected office and even from trying to vote. Any and all means were used from threats to violence to outright murder."*[77] [Other atrocities committed by the Democrats and their Klan supporters are mentioned in previous chapters and more will be covered in subsequent chapters.

For detailed accounts of the Democrats' apathy and terrorist activities from Reconstruction to the Clinton era, see Appendix B, C, H and I, and review Chapters Four, Six, and Eight.]

Today, a number of Democrats proudly boast about their civil rights accomplishment of the sixties, mainly the passage of the 1964 Civil Rights Act. However, after reviewing all the evidence, one must conclude that **had the Democrats passed these same types of laws in 1864, their legislative efforts in 1964 would not have been necessary**. From 1864 and beyond, Democrats proudly legislated Black Codes, Jim Crow laws, and a multitude of other local laws to disenfranchise blacks. These laws were specifically designed to hurt blacks; they passed no laws to help blacks. The underlying truth is this: After two hundred years of racist practices, the Democrats didn't pass laws and develop the programs (in the sixties) because they had a change of heart and fell in love with black folks. They did it because they fell in love with the black vote.

When the Democrats went after the black vote in the sixties, it was a time of social unrest. Riots, protest marches, and militant groups were taking center stage. The nation was in chaos. In 1963, Dr. King drew some 200,000-plus supporters to the Lincoln Memorial to hear his "I Have A Dream" speech. The march was the largest civil rights gathering of its kind at that time. In addition, Dr. King was gaining more support from white voters as he added new issues to his campaign, issues such as gender discrimination, the working class poor, and the Viet Nam War. Dr. King now represented millions of voters, from both black and white citizens. He, and the issues that he represented, could no longer be ignored. The politicians, both Democrat and Republican, didn't see issues; they saw votes. Nixon, Kennedy, and Johnson all took notice. After losing the two previous elections, the Democrats decided to go after the black vote.

Going after the black vote wasn't entirely new for the Democrats. History reveals that since 1870, the Democrats have always gone after the black vote. From 1870 to 1930, the party used fraud, whippings, lynching, murder, intimidation, and mutilation to get their vote. In the 1930s and 1960s they switched from violence and intimidation to manipulation and voter's registration. In their quest to obtain the black vote, Democrats conveniently ignored those portions of history that documented their inhumane treatment of African Americans.

If one would take a close look at history, it would be easy to conclude that the Democrats' primary agenda, as it pertained to blacks, was to either destroy the African American or make him his perpetual servant for profit. The eight black ministers who wrote the August 25, 1888, letter, which can be found in its entirety in the Introduction, used the following words to express or to describe what they felt the Democrats were trying to do to African Americans. They said, *"There seems to be a deep scheme to reduce Negroes of the State to a condition of abject serfdom and peonage."*

According to an investigative article released by Associated Press and published by *The Seattle Times* on December 2, 2001, our black leaders had a right to be suspicious. Associated Press reported that in Southern states and counties controlled by Democrats, black Americans who owned 15 million acres of farmland in 1910 currently own only 2.2 million. The AP reporters said that many blacks lost their land through cheating, intimidation, and even murder. In order to cover up these injustices, which date back to the late 1800's, many Southern courthouses were burned down to destroy the evidence. In view of these facts, the sudden interest in blacks by Democrats during the sixties must be viewed with suspicion.

While some will accept the fact that the Democrats played a major part in building the foundation on which the institution of racism now rests, few are willing to accept the fact that the Republicans formed their party in 1854 to destroy that foundation. While Democrats ignore their history from 1854 to 1934, many of their authors say little to nothing about this period of slavery followed by Reconstruction. A case in point is David L. Cohn's book entitled *The Fabulous Democrats*. His entire book only has a few references regarding slavery. (See pages 29, 63, 64, 66, 67, 70, 73.) None of those references dealt with the brutal treatment of slaves, the intimidation and murder of black voters, or the Democrats' efforts to franchise their slave business into the Northern states. And more important, there were no references regarding a formal apology from the Democratic Party for their past racist practices.[78] See Appendix I.

George Wallace apologized for his racist behavior, and on May 16, 1997, President Clinton gave a formal apology to the black men who were victimized by the Tuskegee Experiment—a government-sponsored program that allowed blacks to die from syphilis. But the records will show that there has never been a formal apology from the Democratic Party for what they did to African Americans during the past two hundred years and for the residual impact that those practices are having on us today.

To praise the Democrats for what they did in the sixties is similar to praising a child who voluntarily cleans up *part* of his mess after tracking mud throughout the entire house. After praising the child, you learn that the child didn't clean up his mess because it was the right thing to do, he did it so he could play video games – a privilege he would not have otherwise received had he not attempted to get rid of the mud. In this analogy, the mud represents the dirty treatment of African Americans by the Democrats, the cleaning represents the token programs of the sixties, and the video games represents what the Democrats really wanted: the White House. Simply put, the Democrats didn't want a relationship with African Americans, they merely wanted **blacks** who could put them in a **White** House.

Reconciliation and healing always begin with an apology and an effort to repay those who have been wronged. In 1973, the government agreed to pay $10 million to more than 6,000 survivors and family members of the Tuskegee Experiment. President Clinton's apology came only after the 20,000 members of the Black National Medical Association asked him for an apology. Clinton said, *"To our African American citizens, I am sorry that your federal government orchestrated a study so clearly racist—that can never happen again."* The Medical Association said, because of the Tuskegee Experiment *"Many blacks have avoided clinical trials for diseases that disproportionately affect them, such as high blood pressure, kidney disease, and cancer."* Some blacks have commented, *"Clinton's apology was the only positive thing he did for blacks during his entire administration."*

One might ask, What about the Republicans? What have they done for blacks recently? Not much, but much more than we give them credit for. The Congressional Quarterly reported that when the 1964 Civil Rights Act came up for vote, Senator Al Gore Sr. and the rest of the Southern Democrats voted against it. In the House, only 61 percent of the Democrats voted for the bill as opposed to 80 percent of the Republicans. In the Senate, only 69 percent of the Democrats voted for it, compared to 82 percent of the Republicans. Many say that if it were not for the efforts of Republican Senator Everett Dirksen of Illinois, the 1964 Civil Rights Act would have never passed. President Lyndon B. Johnson praised him, and the NAACP awarded him. Roy Wilkins, the Chairman of the NAACP at the time, gave the Republican senator the Leadership Conference of Civil Rights Award. Dirksen accepted the award and quietly responded, *"This is an idea whose time has come."*

In more recent years, Republicans didn't promise blacks *anything,* so blacks, as a race didn't receive anything. In fact, in some instances it seemed as if the *modern-day* Republicans were trying to reverse the few political gains that were made during the sixties. During the past three decades, civil rights and equality weren't part of the Republican platform. Reagan and others made it clear that they weren't in favor of the racial quotas and preferences associated with Affirmative Action Programs.

But keep in mind, blacks put the Democrats not the Republicans in office to work for them. No matter how much we may criticize the modern-day Republicans for their lack of sensitivity regarding racial issues today, which seem to be a fact, we cannot ignore the mixed messages we're receiving from today's Democratic Party regarding issues pertaining to blacks. For instance, most black Democrats strongly support reparation pay, while many white Democrats say very little about the subject. Issues regarding reparation pay have been around for some time. Like many politicians today, some supported it and others opposed it.

In 1865, Lincoln wrestled with thoughts regarding those who gained their wealth through slavery. Lincoln, like the white Democrats today, wasn't sure what should be done. But history tells us that he gave considerable thought as to whether or not God was using the war to make some pay for what he called *"the wealth that was piled up by the bondsman's two hundred and fifty years of unrequited toil."* In Volume VI (pages 276-277) of *The Messages and Papers of the Presidents,* Lincoln writes: *"The Almighty has His own purposes. If God wills that it* [the war] *continues until all the wealth piled up by the bondsman's two hundred and fifty years of unrequited toil shall be sunk, and until every drop of blood drawn with the lash shall be paid by another drawn with the sword, as was said three thousand years ago, so still it must be said, 'The judgements of the Lord are true and righteous altogether.'"*[79]

When discussions are raised regarding reparation pay, most confine their discussions to slavery and those who were the benefactors of the free slave labor. Very few of those discussions include the atrocities committed during Reconstruction and beyond, where millions of blacks were murdered, robbed, and denied rights as citizens through Jim Crow laws, Black Codes, and by other repressive legislation. These laws and legislative mandates were specifically designed by the Democratic Party to disenfranchise one ethnic group, the African Americans.

African Americans may ignore many things, but we cannot ignore the Republicans' past efforts to stop the Holocaust of slavery and the horrific racist practices by the Democrats during Reconstruction. The Democrat's legislative actions, segregated practices, and illegal lethal tactics have had a profound negative impact on millions of African Americans during the past twenty decades. As a race, we must remember these two important facts:

1. Despite the Republicans' insensitivity on the racial issues of **today,** they, as a party, have never sponsored

or launched a program, passed laws, or engaged in practices that resulted in the death of *millions* of African Americans.

2. According to leading historians (both black and white), the horrific atrocities committed against African Americans during slavery and Reconstruction were racist activities that were financed, sponsored, and promoted by the Democratic Party and their Klan supporters.

For reasons unknown, many modern-day authors of history have conveniently downplayed or omitted the Democrats' racist past and the Republicans' quest for equality. Consequently, many African Americans are not aware of who did what in their history. According to Tony Brown, *"It is out of ignorance of their own history that many Blacks demean the Republican philosophy and condemn Black Republicans. Blacks have been Republicans historically. Frederick Douglass and the first twelve Blacks to serve as U.S. Congressmen were Republicans. And Congressional White Republicans were the architects of Reconstruction, a ten-year period of unprecedented political power for Black people. Democrats working hand in hand with the Ku Klux Klan gave us Jim Crow Laws that effectively re-enslaved Blacks. If you know this history, you have to wonder: How did Blacks move from the party that gave them civil and political rights to a previously all-White Democratic Party? How did they come to join forces with a party with a history of racist demagoguery, support of slavery, Jim Crow, and lynchings?"*[80]

Modern-Day Republicans and Democrats

This is not to suggest that Republicans of the past were head over heels in love with blacks. Such would be far from the truth. President Rutherford B. Hayes entered into an agreement with racist Democrats, known as the Compromise of 1877, so that he could win the election. Other Republican presidents, such as Lincoln, Theodore Roosevelt, and Taft, felt that blacks were inferior to whites. However, despite their attitudes of superiority and the incident of 1877, Republicans as a whole refused to accept the inhumane treatment that blacks were forced to endure at the hands of those who represented the Democratic Party.

Modern-day Republicans, like their predecessors, must become more racially sensitive. This party, which claims to base their values on Biblical principles, must remember how much God hates racial prejudice. God proved it when He became angry with Moses' sister, Miriam. The Bible records that Miriam was upset because her brother Moses had married a black woman (Numbers 12:1-15). According to the King James version of the Bible, God punished Moses' sister by cursing her and turning her *white as snow* with leprosy. It is ironic that God would punish this woman by turning her *white* because she was angry with a person who married someone **black**. **Modern-day Republicans** must learn from their predecessors who were sensitive enough to start the process of racial equality for African Americans. They must pick up the mantle, embrace the principles of righteousness, and complete the job that their predecessors started.

Modern-day Democrats must stop pretending that they are the compassionate party of black people and confess that it was their predecessors who started many of the racist practices that we are now trying to eradicate. History clearly shows two things: (1) that the roots of racism grew deep in the hearts and souls of the Democrats and (2) without the past efforts of the Radical Republicans and the Abolitionists, the Civil Rights Legislation of the sixties would not have been possible. Republicans laid the foundation for civil rights by passing legislation and instituting programs that Democrats' were adamantly opposed to, such as:

1. **The Thirteenth Amendment in 1865** to abolish slavery.

2. **The Civil Rights Act of 1866** to give Negroes citizenship and protect freedmen from Black Codes and other repressive legislation.

3. **The First Reconstruction Act of 1867** to provide more efficient Government of the Rebel- or Democratic-controlled states.

4. **The Fourteenth Amendment in 1868** to make all persons born in the United States citizens. Part of this Amendment specifically states *"No State shall deprive any person of life, liberty, or property without due process of law; or deny any person within its jurisdiction the equal protection of the laws."*

5. **The Fifteenth Amendment of 1870** to give the right to vote to every citizen.

6. **The Ku Klux Klan Act of 1871** to stop Klan terrorists who terrorized black voters, Republicans, white teachers who taught blacks, and Abolitionists.

7. **The Civil Rights Act of 1875** to protect all citizens in their civil and legal rights and to prohibit racial discrimination in places of public accommodations.

8. **Freedmen Bureau** were social programs established by Republicans to feed, protect, and educate the former slaves.

9. **The 1957 Civil Rights Act** and **the 1960 Civil Rights Acts** were signed into law by President Eisenhower who also established the **U.S. Civil Rights Commission** in 1958, a commission that was rejected by Truman during his administration.

10. **The 1964 Civil Rights Act**, which key Republicans pushed law through while key Southern Democrats like Al Gore Sr. debated against its passage. More Republicans voted for this law than Democrats.

11. **Executive Order 11478** issued by President Nixon on August 8, 1969, to strengthen the **Office of Federal Contract Compliance Programs** (OFCCP). And in 1972, he signed into law **The Equal Employment**

Opportunity Act of 1972, which established the **Equal Employment Opportunities Commission**.
See Appendix H Democrates opposition to Civil Rights Legislation.

Through the Nixon administration, the two agencies (EEOC & OFCCP) became civil rights superpowers. The EEOC Act of 1972 gave the Commission the power to bring class action lawsuits against employers, and Nixon's Executive Order (11478) gave the OFCCP the power to deny government contracts to noncomplying employers. The Order also gave OFCCP the authority to force employers receiving federal funds to set up racial quotas and timetables to meet affirmative action goals.

The *Negro Almanac* states: *"EEOC was strengthened during the 1967-1972 years of Nixon's first term. EEOC's annual budget was raised from $12 million to $42 million and its staff from 250 to 2500. Congress granted EEOC the power to take cases to court....* [Nixon's 1972 Equal Employment Opportunities Act] *also granted EEOC power to bring "Pattern and Practices" lawsuits starting in 1974. Pattern and practices suits usually consist of large class actions against large employers and unions whose hiring, promotions, and seniority policies have been systematic in nature."*

Through the laws and agencies that were established during the Nixon administration, *"AT&T* [in 1973] *entered into a consent decree with EEOC and the Department of Labor. They were required to pay $15 million in* **reparations** *and allocate $23 million each year to raise the pay of blacks and other minorities and women... "*[81] The AT&T consent decree was the largest discrimination settlement in American history at that time. Unfortunately, Nixon's civil rights accomplishments were overshadowed by the scandal of Watergate.

Without the key pieces of legislation passed by various Republican administrations, there would be no civil rights as we know them today. The facts presented in this chapter may convince some, that when it comes to civil rights, the Republicans have as much to boast about as the Democrats.

President Richard Nixon
He introduced goals and timetables to assure
Affirmative Action.

Today both parties are overlooking their past. One party is overlooking the terrible things they did to blacks. The other party is overlooking the terrific things they did for blacks. One party literally gave their lives to hurt us, the other gave their lives to help us. Both parties must remember their past. One needs to remember its past to correct the things they did to us and the other needs to remember their past to continue the things they did for us.

In conclusion, both Democrats and Republicans must work together. Neither party is in the position to cast stones at each other (See Appendix F). Both sides must *"come and reason together"* (Isaiah1:18) and work on these problems as sensible, and hopefully godly, men and women. The September 11th terrorist attack on New York and Washington, D.C., proved that parties can put aside their differences and work together harmoniously, in a godly fashion. This was a time when no one thought about race, color, or political affiliation. It was a time when we cried together, prayed together, and sung together in harmony, *"God Bless America."*

We do not need more politics nor do we need more politicians, Black or White. We need elected officials who are committed to using **godly** principles, such as *loving our neighbor* to eliminate all forms of racism and social problems that will benefit all people. Our collective faith in God has been a positive influence in our past and it can be a positive influence in our future, if we once again choose to rely on it.

Chapter Eight

Faith-Based Programs
We Did It Before; We Can Do It Again

Although most historians do not want to admit it, faith and reliance on God has always shaped our history and played an important part in many of the social changes in America. See Appendix G 1787-1802. Inspired by faith, Christians and Catholics built hospitals, schools, youth organizations, orphanages, and the famous Underground Railroad. These faith-based programs made us a great nation. If we, as a nation, can put aside partisan politics and once again put our faith in God, we can again become a great people, a great country, and perhaps regain the important traditional values that we discarded along the way.

Faith-based programs, or programs initiated by Christians and other religious faiths, are not new. In times past, it wasn't the government that launched many of the social programs that we enjoy today—it was the Christian Church. Today a number of churches continue the traditional role of the church of yesterday by sponsoring and financing relevant faith-based programs to meet the social and spiritual needs of their community.

One of the most powerful faith-based programs ever launched was the Abolitionist Movement. Speaking of the Abolitionist Movement, Professor James McPherson said, *"Most historians have paid little attention to the abolitionist movement after 1860.... Early in the war, abolitionists outlined a broad program of emancipation, employment of Negro soldiers in the Union Army, creation of a Freedman Bureau, government assistance for the education of the freedmen, civil and political equality for all black men, and grants of confiscated land to the freed slaves. Under military pressures of war and the political pressures of the Reconstruction, the Republican Party adopted all of these policies....* "[82]

Many historians are now acknowledging that a great number of the abolitionists were inspired by their Christian faith, and many gave their lives for the cause. When placed on trial for his 1859 raid on the federal arsenal at Harper's Ferry, Virginia, abolitionist John Brown said these words just before his execution. *"Had I interfered in the manner on behalf of the rich, the powerful, and the intelligent, every man in this court would have deemed it an act worthy of reward. But I interfered on behalf of God's despised poor. I did no wrong, but right."*

In one of his final letters Brown wrote: *"I commend you all to Him whose mercy endureth forever, to the God of my fathers whose I am and whom I serve. He will never leave you nor forsake you. Finally, my dearly beloved, be of good comfort. Be sure to remember and follow my advice, and my example too, so far as it has been consistent with the holy religion of Jesus Christ, in which I remain a most firm and humble believer. Never forget the poor, nor think anything in them to be lost in you, even though they may be black as Ebedmelech, the Ethiopian eunuch who cared for Jeremiah in the pit of the dungeon; or as black as the one to whom Philip preached Christ. Here, before God, in the presence of these witnesses, I consecrate my life to the destruction of Slavery."* [83]

Under the Fugitive Slave Laws, abolitionists and their children were harassed, beaten and even murdered for assisting runaways slaves. The law also permitted the confiscation of land, homes, and other property to discourage participation in the Underground Railroad, but it did not discourage individuals like Levi Coffin, a white Quaker who was considered to be the president of the Underground Railroad. To discourage Arthur Tappan, a wealthy white retailer from New York, they burned his home, cancelled his bank loans, cancelled his insurance policy on his business, and cancelled shipments on the products he ordered. When they offered to reinstate all that was taken from him if he would resign from the New York Anti-Slavery Society, he responded, *"I'll hang first."*

By 1832, over 400,000 persons were members of the various anti-slavery societies, and they were committed to doing everything within their power to assist the runaway slaves.

Hannah Gibbons hid slaves on her small farm because she said the Bible told her *"to love her neighbors."*

Attorney Isaac Tatum Hopper successfully defended hundreds of runaway slaves in the Northern courts of law. John Rankin and his seven sons were attacked by pro-slavery mobs over one hundred times for their participation in the Underground Railroad.

Dr. Alexander Ross, a rich, prominent, and renowned Northern doctor, infiltrated the South during his lecture tours, only to arm slaves with guns, food, and compasses to aid in their escape from the plantations.

In 1775, abolitionist and former slave trader John Newton was sent word from the University of New Jersey that the school made him an honorary Doctor of Divinity. He turned down the honor and stated that, because of his involvement in the slave trade, he would *"never accept any diploma, except it came from poor Blacks."* One day, with a repentant heart he sat down and wrote these words:

> *"Amazing grace how sweet the sound.*
> *That saved a wretch like me.*
> *I once was lost, but now I'm found,*
> *Was blind but now I see."*

These individuals represent thousands of unsung heroes who were inspired by their faith to fight against those people, primarily Democrats who wanted to expand their slave trade business into the new Northern states. The Abolitionist Movement was perhaps one of the most successful faith-based programs in American history. This is not to say that all abolitionists were Christians, but a vast majority of them were, including Susan B. Anthony, a Quaker, who was inspired by her abolitionist father.

While Susan devoted much of her time and attention to fighting for women's rights, children of other abolitionists continued their parents' work by providing education and new legislation for the newly freed slaves. Several of these individuals worked with the American Missionary Association (AMA), a faith-based organization dedicated to opening new schools in the South to educate the American Negro. Professor James McPherson reports that when the AMA sent white teachers to Southern communities to educate Negroes, the old-time Southern hospitality was immediately transformed into Southern hostility.

Professor McPherson said: "*Southern hostility to Yankee teachers sometimes went beyond ostracism and verbal abuse. In times of political excitement during Reconstruction, many missionaries were threatened, beaten, and murdered. The AMA reported several incidents similar to the one in which a group of masked men took a teacher from his house in North Carolina in 1874, tied him up, and after threatening to kill him if he did not leave the state, gave him 100 lashes with a bullwhip. The founder and president for nearly 30 years of Shaw University, Henry Tupper of Massachusetts, was often harassed by the Ku Klux Klan and once hid all night in a cornfield with his wife and two children to avoid an assassination attempt.*

"*In 1871, a college treasurer went to a nearby town on business, had dinner with a Black family, and after leaving a prayer meeting at a Negro church was ambushed by five men who fired at him seven times and left him for dead. The shots had missed, however, the treasurer returned to his hotel, where at 3:00 AM 30 masked men dragged him from his bed, took him to the woods, and gave him 61 lashes with a hickory whip.*

"*The 1874 elections were a particularly tense time; as one teacher put it, to be for weeks in a constant expectation of being murdered or burned out, and without losing faith in God, is something of a strain on the nerves.*

"*In 1879, the Northern Methodists compiled a list of 34 attacks on their missionaries and teachers in the past decade; 19 of the victims were white and 15 black, three of the whites and four of the Blacks were killed.*

"The AMA tried for several years to cooperate with local [Southern] school boards. So long as <u>Republicans</u> were in power this arrangement worked out reasonably well. But when the <u>Democrats</u> began to regain control of the South the dual support foundered and eventually collapsed. In Memphis the <u>Democrats</u> dismissed all AMA teachers, forcing the association to withdraw from the jointly sponsored Lincoln School and founded LeMoyne Institute in its place. In Columbus, Mississippi, <u>Democrats</u> drove out the Union Academy's Northern teachers with threats of violence and then closed the school in 1871."[84]

Abolitionist Influence on NAACP and Negro Colleges

While the violence discouraged some, others were more determined. The determined ones included John D. Rockefeller and Oswald Garrison Villard. Many of us may have heard of billionaire John D. Rockefeller and possibly even Oswald Garrison Villard, but few have heard about their work on behalf of blacks, particularly in the areas of social justice and education. Oswald Garrison Villard and Mary White Ovington, who came from a long line of abolitionists, were the original founders and directors of the NAACP, and John D. Rockefeller was the Republican philanthropist who donated millions of dollars to black colleges.

In reference to Villard and Ovington's work, historian John Hope Franklin said, *"In 1909, liberal whites such as Mary White Ovington, Oswald Garrison Villard, and William English Walling issued a call for a conference to consider the plight of African Americans."*[85] In that same year, these key individuals met and formed what is now known as the NAACP or the National Association for the Advancement of Colored People. In confirming Professor Franklin's findings, the *Negro Almanac* reports that the formation of the *"NAACP was largely the brain-child of Ovington, Villard, and Walling, three white individuals."*[86]

By 1936, these individuals and other white liberals continued to play a major role in the NAACP, focusing primarily on eliminating the lynching of black citizens. According to Juan Williams, author of *Thurgood Marshall: American Revolutionary*, as the organization grew, the NAACP depended heavily on white Republican philanthropist for its financial support.

Although the work of Ovington, Villard, and Walling was very significant, they and other well deserving white Republicans are often overlooked in the chronicles of black history. Such is the case with Henry L. Morehouse and Laura Spelman, two white individuals who worked very hard to establish and maintain some of our historical black colleges.

Laura Spelman's work with black schools and colleges had a profound influence on both her husband and her son, John D. Rockefeller and John D. Rockefeller Jr. In 1902, father and son set up a General Education Board to assist Southern black schools. By the end of the first decade, the board had donated over $33,000,000 toward furthering the goals of black education. By 1921, they had donated an additional $96,000,000 for education, and black schools and colleges were the recipients of some of this money as well. Spelman College, established for African American women, bears the name of this devout Christian woman who was also the daughter of an abolitionist father.

Henry L. Morehouse was the Executive Secretary of the Home Mission Society, an organization that financed and started many of the first black schools and colleges. Morehouse received national recognition when a prominent black college in Atlanta, Georgia, the Augusta Institute, decided to honor him by naming their school after him (Morehouse College). All of these individuals were either devout abolitionists or Radical Republicans who were dedicated to helping blacks achieve equality through quality education. Many prominent African American leaders were the benefactors of these faith-based schools and the funding provided by Christian and Republican philanthropists. Dr. Martin Luther King graduated from Morehouse College and it is reported that the Rev. Jesse Jackson received a scholarship from the Rockefeller Fund to attend Chicago Theological Seminary.

During Reconstruction, educating the newly freed slaves was also a high priority for other faith-based groups and missionary societies. Again, McPherson tells us, *"Baptist freedmen's schools were sustained at first mainly by New England abolitionists in the denomination. When Henry L. Morehouse became secretary of the Home Mission Society in 1879, he made black education the society's main work. Morehouse served as executive secretary from 1879 to 1893, field secretary from 1893 to 1902, and executive secretary again from 1902 until his death in 1917. Thomas Morgan was executive secretary from 1893 to 1902. Both men came to maturity as abolitionists in the turbulent 1850's; Morgan commanded four regiments of black troops in the war.*

"By 1870 most of the Quaker societies were supporting 47 elementary and six secondary schools. Many of the first and second generation abolitionists who went South as founders, presidents, principals, and teachers of freedmen's schools spent the rest of their lives in this work."

*The two presidents who built **Howard University** from a struggling institution to the foremost black university in the country were lifelong abolitionists: William W. Patton was president from 1877 to 1889 and died in office; Jeremiah E. Rankin served from 1890 to 1903, dying a year after his retirement. Wilbur P. Thirkield was president of Howard from 1906 to 1912.*

Atlanta University's *founder and first president (1867-1885) was Edmund Asa Ware, who had been converted to abolitionism as a young man by reading* Uncle Tom's Cabin. *The founder of **Fisk University** was Erastus M. Cravath. Cravath had been brought up by an abolitionist father and had attended two integrated colleges, New York Central College and Oberlin. He had been American Missionary Association's district and field secretary for 10 years before assuming the presidency of Fisk.*

*Abolitionists who headed Methodist schools included George Whipple Hubbard of **Meharry Medical College**. Joseph Robert, a Southerner who left his native section in 1850 because he hated slavery, became the first president of **Morehouse College**, which was an institution that had three name changes and one location change.*

In 1915, the editor of the Negro Year Book *estimated that over the past half century Northern sources had contributed **$57 million** to Negro education and blacks themselves had provided an additional **$24 million**."*[87]

Black Colleges

The following is a list of a few black schools and colleges started by various missionary societies of the North. Again, these schools were financed, funded, and sponsored by prominent Republicans and their abolitionist supporters, while the Democrats, with brutal force, opposed every effort these two groups put forth to educate the American Negro.

School	Date	Place
Morehouse College	1867	Atlanta, GA
Howard University	1867	Washington, D.C.
Spelman Seminary	1881	Atlanta, GA
Shaw University	1865	Raleigh, NC
Fisk University	1866	Nashville, TN
Atlanta University	1867	Atlanta, GA
Virginia Union University	1899	Richmond, VA
Straight University	1869	New Orleans, LA
Talladega College	1867	Talladega, AL
Clark University	1870	Atlanta, GA
Meharry Medical College	1876	Nashville, TN
Morgan College	1867	Baltimore, MD

New Orleans University	1873	New Orleans, LA
Philander Smith College	1883	Little Rock, AR
Rust College	1883	Holy Springs, MS
Samuel Houston College	1900	Austin, TX

According to Professor J. Owen Smith, professor of Afro-Ethnic Studies for California State University at Fullerton, Democrats were a problem during Reconstruction and they were also a problem during the Johnson, Carter, and Bush (George H.W.) administrations. Smith said, *"It was under the Johnson and Carter administrations and later during the Bush administration that an effort was made to destroy black colleges. When the effort was pushed under Nixon and Ford, their position was to keep your hands off of the black colleges. Under Carter, the effort to desegregate the black colleges* [or lose government funding] *resurfaced. But when the issue came up during the Bush administration, he abandoned the idea and pledged to allocate more money for the Historical Black Colleges. Without the Black Colleges, the number of black student graduates would drop significantly."*

Lasting Faith-Based Programs

The Abolitionist Movement, with their efforts to educate the newly freed slaves, was just one of many faith-based programs that have touched the lives of millions. Little do we realize just how many of today's social programs were started by individuals who were inspired by their faith to meet the needs of others, both black and white. Listed below are just a few of the people and their programs.

In an effort to improve the spiritual development of young men, George Williams started in 1842 what is known today as the Young Men's Christian Association or the YMCA. Thirteen years later, in 1855, the YWCA was formed for women. Their social programs include recreation, education, housing, and feeding the poor. During the past 150 years, hundreds of millions have passed through their doors.

In 1865, a Methodist minister founded a program to feed and house the poor. His name was William Booth and his program was The Salvation Army. In addition to preaching the gospel, this organization continues to provide a multitude of faith-based social services in over eighty countries throughout the world. Their 16,000 centers and 3,000-plus social welfare institutions, hospitals, and schools have provided food, shelter, health care, and education for millions.

In 1917, Father Edward J. Flanagan, a Catholic priest from Nebraska, formed a faith-based organization to provide a home for orphaned and homeless boys. The 1500-acre site was called Boys Town. Housing over 1,000 children, the site became a self-sufficient village with its own farms and schools. Thousands of young men have passed through their doors during the past eighty-four years.

On February 7, 1837, a young girl from a very rich family in London heard the voice of God. She said the Lord told her that He had a special mission for her. Her name was Florence Nightingale. Seventeen years later, in 1854, she went to war to assist the victims of war. Inspired by her faith in God, she spent over $100,000 of her own money to help the wounded soldiers. In 1860, she opened the Nightingale School for Nurses to train young women. This woman of faith is not only the mother of the nursing profession, her efforts and vision have had and will continue to have a direct impact on hundreds of millions of people around the world.

On June 24, 1859, after seeing 40,000 causalities during the war, Jean Henri Dunant, a devout Christian from Geneva, Switzerland, started what evolved into a worldwide faith-based program to help those who were victimized by war and other types of disasters: the Red Cross. Because the cross is the symbol of Christianity, the Muslim chapters replaced the cross symbol with a red crescent. Even though the two organizations use different symbols, they, along with the Salvation Army, all came together after the September 11, 2001, terrorist attack and became the primary care providers for the victims and their families.

Long before the government ever thought about health care, most of the private hospitals in America were inspired, funded, and operated by Protestant and Catholic organizations. It was a faith-based hospital that provided care for the victims of the September 11 terrorist attack on New York's Twin Towers. News reports indicate that St. Vincent Catholic hospital had as many as 500 doctors on hand and treated over 1200 patients during the first twenty-four hour period of the terrorist attack. According to the chronicles of history, some of the oldest hospitals in America, like St. Vincent, are rooted in Christianity.

Around the world, the archives of history hold the most inspiring stories of individuals who were motivated by their faith to make a difference in their lives and in the lives of others. No where is this more evident than in black history.

Chapter Nine

Doing Things for Ourselves

Blacks Who Made A Difference vs
Blacks Who Made Excuses

Problems, heartaches, and pains have seemingly been the plight and experience of every African American since we first stepped onto American soil. The realities of our struggles are documented not only in the chronicles of Black History, but in American History as well. The injustices that we faced produced pain, the pain produced problems, and the problems produced two types of African Americans: those who put their **faith in God** and made a difference, and those who simply **ignored God** and made excuses.

Blacks who made a difference, trusted God, turned their stumbling blocks into stepping stones, and built a stairway to success. Others who simply made excuses did not see the blocks as stepping stones, but as obstacles to their future. Thus many became angry, bitter, and self-abusive. Instead of viewing the blocks as a means that could take them from the Valley of Despair to the Plateaus of Prosperity, they viewed them as worthless materials and used them to build a Monument of Excuses—excuses that eventually destroyed their families, their homes, their communities, their values, and eventually themselves.

In contrast, those who made a difference were able to do so because they put their trust in God, took the same materials, and made a multitude of differences. They made products out of peanuts, schools out of churches, and political spokesmen out of preachers. When the stumbling blocks kept blacks out of white restaurants and hotels, they didn't complain; instead, they built their own restaurants and hotels. When the blocks prevented blacks from joining major league baseball teams, Buck O'Neil, director of the Negro Baseball Museum, says, *"They didn't complain."* They used these blocks and formed the Negro Baseball League, a league that *"drew more fans than their white counterparts."* When major insurance companies would not insure blacks, they seized the opportunity and started their own insurance companies, such as the North Carolina Mutual Insurance Company. When the blocks of racism prevented blacks from joining various organizations and associations, they took advantage of these obstacles and started their own organizations like the National Bar Association and the National Negro Business League. And when major news organizations refused to cover events in the black community, they built their own news organizations like the *Pittsburgh Courier*, *The Chicago Defender*, and *The Negro Digest*.

The stumbling blocks that we face today are the same types of stumbling blocks our great-grandparents faced during their day. The biggest difference between their generation and our generation was their faith in God and their determination to make a difference.

Taking Responsibility to Do for Ourselves

In the late 1800s, Booker T. Washington started a series of Negro Conferences. During one conference in 1896, the following were his opening remarks regarding the need for blacks to do things for themselves.

"The aim will be, as in the four previous years, to bring together for a quiet conference, <u>not politicians</u>, but the representatives of the common, hard working farmers and mechanics and <u>the backbone and sinew of the Negro race</u>, the <u>ministers and teachers</u>. I want to emphasize the object of these conferences. When they were first instituted, it was to confine ourselves mainly to the conditions within <u>our own power to remedy</u>. We might discuss many wrongs which should be righted; but it seems to me that it is best to

lay hold of the things we can put right rather than those we can do nothing but find fault with. To be perfectly frank with each other; state things as they are; do not say anything for mere sound, or because you think it will please one or displease another; let us hear the truth on all matters. We have many things to discourage and disappoint us, and we sometimes feel that we are slipping backwards; but I believe, if we do our duty in getting property, Christian education, and character, in some way or other the sky will clear up, and we shall make our way onward."[88]

One hundred and six years later, columnist William Raspberry of *The Washington Post* expressed similar feelings during an interview with *Newsweek* magazine. On April 6, 1992, *Newsweek* reported that Raspberry said, *"Black Americans are still captives of the sixties and its political goals. Racism and poverty are not the reasons why we are in the situation we are in today. To try to link our solutions to elective politics is to put government on the hook for things we should do ourselves."*[89]

Far too many people are waiting for the government or a particular political party to do what we can do ourselves. This is not to say that as voters and taxpayers we do not have the right to demand certain things from our government and our political representatives. We do have this right and we should exercise this right. After all, it is we, the taxpayers, who employ these individuals to work for us. With our tax dollars we provide both the salaries and the physical offices that they occupy, for both the Democrats and the Republicans.

African Americans should never be too embarrassed to ask for government funding—our tax dollars—to develop self-help programs for our people. Contrary to what many are led to believe, major corporations are the biggest benefactors of our tax dollars, not our nation's welfare recipients. We often overlook the fact that our government purchases tanks, planes, desks, chairs, computers, copiers, and millions of other items from the private sector, i.e., corporations. Each day, these corporations compete for our tax dollars through their powerful lobbyists. In 1968 there were only sixty-two registered lobbyists in Washington, D.C.; in 2002, there are *20,000*, all lobbying for our tax dollars to fund corporate programs and projects.   If corporate America isn't embarrassed or afraid to ask for our tax dollars to benefit themselves and their stockholders, as African American taxpayers, we shouldn't be embarrassed to make those same requests on behalf of our people. Any money coming from the government is merely a rebate of what we have already given them.   Without our taxes, the government has no money to give.

Request for government funding should be made regardless of which political party is in power.   Dr. King held both parties accountable and we should do the same.   After dealing with President John F. Kennedy (Democrat), and learning that (Democratic) President Lyndon B. Johnson referred to him (Dr. King) as *"that nigger preacher,"* Dr. King realized two things: **one, that racism was not limited to one political party and two, that modern day civil rights' legislation <u>must have</u> bipartisan support to pass**. Congressional debates in Appendix H supports Dr. King's conclusion regarding bi-partisanship support.   Congressional records also reveal that **African Americans have enemies and allies in <u>both</u> political parties**. African Americans, like Dr. King (and all other political interest groups), must embrace their allies and reject their enemies, regardless of whether the person(s) is a member of the Democratic Party or the Republican Party.

Dr. King was invited to the White House during President Eisenhower's administration and he was also invited to the White House during the Kennedy/Johnson administrations. He played a major role in bringing about social change and major civil rights legislation because he was willing to work with both parties.

We not only have the responsibility to hold both parties accountable, we must be willing to do what our people did in the past.   They trusted in God and their God-given gifts and talents, then used their faith and talents to make a difference.   We cannot stand around expecting others to do what we can do for ourselves.

In the Afterword of Dr. King's book, *Why We Can't Wait*, the Rev. Jesse Jackson said: *"Had Dr. King waited for an elected official or a politician to be bold enough to do the right thing and change the law to include every American in the American Dream, change would have never come. Dr. King knew that the key to unlocking American Apartheid was not in the White House or any governor's mansion. It was in the homes of average citizens. Dr. King knew that if the people stood up and used their collective power, they could change an entire nation. So home by home, congregation by congregation, city by city, Dr. King convinced the people that they had the power if only they would use it."*[90]

Another unknown author put it this way:

"There was an important job to be done and Everybody was sure that Somebody would do it. Anybody could have done it, but Nobody did it. Somebody got angry about that, because it was Everybody's job. Everybody thought Anybody could do it, but Nobody realized that Everybody wouldn't do it. It ended up that Everybody blamed Somebody when Nobody did what Anybody could have done."

Both Jesse Jackson and Al Sharpton would probably agree that they are not the ones who are really making a difference in our communities, it is the millions of *"Nobodies, Anybodies,* and *Everybodies"* (selfless volunteers) who give their time to support a variety of community-based social programs. Those programs include coaching, tutoring, and mentoring inner-city youth as well as preparing both youth and adults for college, new careers, and better-paying jobs.

Although the work of these volunteers is significant, our communities are in desperate need of many more volunteers. Each year, Bank of America responds to this need with hundreds of their own employee volunteers through their Leadership Excellence in Neighborhood Development (LEND) Program. The volunteers are led by the bank's own CEO, Hugh McColl. In the year 2000, Hugh led a group of 250 bank employees to Marshall Heights Community Center in Washington, D.C. With hammers, nails, picks, and shovels in hand, they transformed the worn-down community center into a modern-day wonder in just one day.

A question one might ask is, How many times did the members of the Congressional Black Caucus pass by this community center and ignored its condition? The 250 **bank executives** weren't residents of Washington, D.C.; they came from all parts of the country to work on the project. During the past seven years, the bank, through its LEND program, has completed similar projects in other states, including the renovation of the Satchel Paige Baseball Field in Kansas, near the historic Negro Baseball Museum.

African Americans do not need leaders who will merely use their lips to lecture in the legislature. They need leaders who will lend a helping hand to change their community. Every black leader, politician, professional athlete, and entertainer should return to their community once a year and put on work clothes and physically do something to improve their community. Like the executives of Bank of America and former president Jimmy Carter, who builds homes for low-income citizens, our leaders and celebrities must forget their status and get involved in a variety of community-based projects. Projects that include cleaning up neighborhoods; building teen centers; tutoring; serving the needy; painting and remodeling recreational facilities, schools, and senior citizens' homes; and assisting single parents with their children and teachers with their classes. We must always remember that beautiful, peaceful communities are not legislated into existence. These types of communities are built and developed by the dedicated members of the community. If a former president of the United States can take the time to physically build homes for the poor in our communities, we have no excuse.

In addition to being involved in community-based projects, African Americans must keep in mind that practical manifestations without spiritual transformation cannot and will not solve the negative behavioral and attitudinal problems that are destroying our youth, our families, and our communities. We must have a well-thought-out, balanced approach to our problems and our solutions must include a spiritual component.

Chapter Ten

Walking by the Same Rule

The Solution

How do we solve the pressing problems facing Black Americans? Some believe we need a spiritual revival; others believe education is the solution. And then there are those who feel blacks need to spend less and invest more in their community. It is obvious that our problems are not the result of not having enough churches, schools, and money. According to *Christianity Today* magazine, the black community has over 37,000 local churches and an annual income that exceeds 36 billion dollars. Economist Andrew F. Brommer reports, as consumers, *"Blacks spend more than $500 billion dollars a year,"* roughly the equivalent to the gross domestic product of Canada or Australia, but they have little to show for it.

Perhaps the prophet Hosea was right. Maybe our problems are the result of not having the proper knowledge. The Bible says, *"Our people are destroyed because of a lack of knowledge"* (Hosea 4:6). What type of knowledge was Hosea referring to? To the Jews it meant:

1. Knowledge of God and His promises and principles
2. Knowledge of their culture and their history
3. Knowledge of the powerful secular cultures that surround them
4. Knowledge of the government system that governed them

5. Knowledge of finance and business practices and principles
6. Knowledge of each other and what works best for them as a race
7. Knowledge of God's law and man's laws

As we consider solutions, our solutions must include God. James Weldon Johnson refers to Him as the *"God of our silent tears,* the *God of our weary years*, the one *who has brought us thus far on the way.* The God *who by His might, led us into the light,* the one *who will keep us forever in the path* [when] *we pray."*

Johnson's words seem to suggest that, to move forward, we, like the Jews, must have a strong sense of history, meaning where we come from, and a clear understanding of the God who played a major part in our success. Johnson realized that it was our faith in God that gave us a sense of unity, unity that caused us to support one another economically, emotionally, and spiritually. His poem calls for the realization of our past, spiritual guidance for the present, and staying on the right *path* for our future.

A quick review of history will reveal that it wasn't money that provided peace and stability in our community. We had far less money than we have today, but we were more caring, more supportive, and more law-abiding. We had stronger families, stronger values and a much stronger faith in God. These were the times that young Sean Conner referred to in his letter to Dr. King. To return to those times or to the mindset we had during those times, we must rebuild on the foundation that our predecessors laid for us. That foundation was God's Word—the Bible.

A Rule Book for Unity

The Bible established one unbiased standard for all to live by. It was the rule book that governed our community, our business practices, as well as our individual behavior toward one another.

We supported each other and other black institutions, because the Bible told us: *"Two are better than one"* (Ecclesiastes 4:9); *"to be kindly affectionate to one another"* (Romans 12:10); and that *"a house divided against itself cannot stand"* (Matthew 12:25). Community support was evident everywhere: in our schools, in our churches, and in our social events.

Buck O'Neil, the founder and Executive Director of the Negro Baseball Museum said: *"When the Negro Baseball players came to town, members of black churches would open their homes to give the players a place to stay."* And that wasn't all. *"Pastors would dismiss church early so their members could pack family lunches and attend the games."* From these types of biblically based concepts of unity and support, we started schools, insurance companies, banks, savings and loan institutions, and a multitude of other businesses. At one time, we had over 100,000 members in the National Negro Business League. Booker T. Washington, who started the Negro Business League, felt that economic prosperity was also an answer to his mother's prayers.

In times past, we looked out for one another because the Bible told us to *"love our neighbor"* (Matthew 22:40). When the mother next door became ill, loving our neighbor meant going to our neighbor's home, cooking their meals, washing their clothes, cleaning their home, and nursing the ill mother back to health. Loving our neighbor included everything from helping to deliver babies to delivering boxes of groceries when our neighbor fell on hard times. These were the things that we were taught to do through the black church.

In years past, the black church, not the U.S. Government, was the key to meeting the social and spiritual needs of the community. The black church must take on some of those responsibilities again. Gregory Reed, attorney and author of *Economic Empowerment Through the Church*, says, *"The black church was the backbone for African American entrepreneurs."* Reed acknowledged, *"After slavery was abolished, 240 banks were started and blacks owned some 20 million acres of land"* and the black church played a major part in this achievement. He said, *"Today there are fewer than 30 banks and our land ownership has been reduced to less than 2.2 million acres."*[91]   Emmett D. Carson, author *of A Hand Up; Black Philanthropy and Self-Help in America*, says, *"Billions of dollars a year is channeled through the black church through its tithes and offerings. This represents 90% of black giving and makes the black church the one enduring institution in low-income black communities with the ability to secure major credit."*[92]

Many are convinced that the key to solving our problems is the black church. As goes the black church, so goes the community. The problems in the community mirror the problems in the church. If the church is self-centered and lacks compassion, the same is often reflected in the community. Some believe the division of our youth by gang affiliation, the lack of student volunteers in community services, and the disrespect that we have for one another, as heard through our music, *may* be a reflection of what is going on in many of today's inner-city churches.

The church must play a major part in the solution process, as it did in Queens, New York, under Rev. Floyd Flake's leadership. However, it will be impossible for the church to fulfill its role if we remain divided by political parties and continue to fight and bicker among ourselves. We must be more loyal to our Lord, than to our legislators and more loyal to our church and our people than we are to our politicians. Frederick Douglass said it best, when he spoke at the 1883 National Convention of Colored Men in Louisville, Kentucky:

> *"If six million of colored people of this country, armed with the Constitution of the United States, with a million votes of their own to lean upon, and millions of white men at their back, whose hearts are responsive to the claims of humanity, have not sufficient spirit and wisdom to <u>organize</u> and <u>combine</u> to defend themselves from outrage, discrimination, and oppression, it will be idle for them to expect that the Republican party or any other political party will organize and combine for them*

or care what becomes of them. Men may combine to prevent cruelty to animals, for they are dumb and cannot speak for themselves; but we are men and must speak for ourselves, or we shall not be spoken for at all. Parties were made for men, not men for parties."[93]

Douglass's words are as relevant today as they were in 1883. In addition to understanding the need to *"combine"* or unite, we must always remember that there can be no unity if there are no general standards to establish guidelines for unity. The Bible tells us four important things to achieve unity and success:

1. Amos 3:3 tells us, *"How can two walk together except they agree?"* We must reach an agreement on our common goals and objectives and strive together to obtain them.

2. Philippians 3:13 tells us, *"Forgetting those things which are behind and press for the higher calling in Christ Jesus."* We must forget our past mistakes and embrace the higher calling of loving one another as Christians.

3. Philippians 3:16 tells us to *"Walk by the same rule and mind the same things."* We must be governed by one set of rules and have the same common interest in our overall welfare.

4. St. John 15:5 says, *"Without me [Jesus] you can do nothing."* We must realize that the God of the universe and the Creator of all things is our most powerful resource for success—not the political parties.

Finally, we must depend more on our Christ-centered preachers than on our crisis-oriented politicians. In his interview with *Playboy* magazine, Dr. King put it this way: *"I talked to many groups,*

Fredrick Douglass
An abolitionist who urged blacks not to depend solely upon political
parties for their destiny.

including one group of 200 ministers. I stressed that the Negro minister had particular freedom and independence to provide strong, firm leadership, and I asked how the Negro would ever gain free-dom without his minister's guidance, support, and inspiration."[94]

In Conclusion

The African American culture did not evolve by accident. It was meticulously developed and designed through the wisdom and leadership of the black clergy. Using the Bible as their guide, they selected from the Western culture those cultural components that they thought were best for their people and built a culture within a culture. The impact they had on the African American cannot be denied or ignored, nor can we ignore the powerful influence that such men and women maintain today.

The black clergyman was not a magician or a man born with extraordinary power. He was merely an ordinary man who was empowered by his faith in God. Without God, he was hopeless and helpless. The wisdom that he expressed came from God. The courage that he possessed came from God, and the foundation on which he rested came from God.

It was God—through His divine word, the Bible—that inspired the black clergy to build churches, open up schools and colleges, and encourage members to start new businesses. Then God told them to boldly stand up for righteousness and challenge social injustice.

The black clergy was the spiritual gardener who planted seeds of righteousness in the fertile hearts of black men and women. And from those seeds grew a strong culture and a strong people, rooted in righteousness and grounded in God, a people who looked to God for everything and based all of their commitments on *"if it's the Lord's will"* (James 4:15).

Through the planting and pruning of God's gardeners, African Americans blossomed into a beautiful culture, one with strong morals, strong family values, and a strong faith in God.

Today, our cultural garden, as we once knew it, is all but destroyed. Many of our spiritual gardeners have lost the art of planting and pruning, while others are trading their pruning shears and plows for politics, and studying preaching no more.

Today, our cultural garden is filled with weeds, weeds that produce gang violence, alcoholism, drugs, teenage pregnancy, and broken homes. The flowers that once blossomed with pride in the African American paradise are now starting to wither while others are being rooted up by nonreligious government programs and by ministers who are compromising godly standards for a status in society. Isaiah referred to these individuals as "*greedy dumb dogs*," who have lost their boldness to bark (Isaiah 56:10-11).

Our cultural garden doesn't look the same anymore. It seems as if everyone is taking advantage of our cultural experience and planting everything in our garden except those things that made us a strong people. The old time black minister is **rarely** seen around the garden anymore. He has been replaced with representatives from the women's movement, the gay rights movement, and every other group that has claimed they can identify with us, all planting their own ideas and agendas. There are so many people in our garden, there's hardly room for us, and none are interested in planting our cultural seeds—seeds that produced God-fearing people, strong families, and a race of people with high moral standards. The beautiful species we once knew seems to no longer exist.

We must do something and we must do it now. We must learn of our culture before we can appreciate our culture, and we must appreciate our culture before we can preserve our culture. We must not allow others to destroy our cultural beauty, nor can we remain passive and allow others to give us an identity that separates us from the God who has done so much for us (Hosea 6:1).

We must embrace our own beauty and cherish our own identity. We must never allow others to devalue those things that made us so wonderfully unique. And we must never allow others to determine our destiny, when they have never been a part of our dignity.

Author's Final Comments

As I stated in the Introduction, I am certainly not one who is without fault or one who is in the position to cast stones at others. The purpose of this fact-finding investigation is not to condemn or endorse, nor to hurt or to harm, but rather to provide truth. I do not believe that leaders and politicians (whether Republican or Democrat) are cold, callous individuals who have lost the compassion and capacity to care. I believe that, in a status-oriented society, it is very easy to lose sight of reality and start focusing on our personal status rather than on our God-given mission to care for one another. I think all of us—whether preacher, politician, professional athlete, or professional entertainer—must be reminded of where we have come from, so we can fully understand where we need to go.

We must be reminded of times when we had no status, times when the only persons who knew us were family and friends in our community. Times when we were hungry and longed for the day when we could wear new clothes rather than mere hand-me-downs. Times when our parents found creative ways to make dinner from welfare canned meat and school sandwiches from welfare cheese and peanut butter. Times when our favorite drink wasn't champagne or fine wine, but red Kool Aid and ice-cold lemonade.

Remembering those times has a way of reminding us of our God-given mission *to love our neighbors as ourselves.* Those were the times when small children dreamed of meeting real movie stars and their favorite athletes. Now we have become the movie stars, the professional athletes, the corporate executives and the politicians whom we once dreamed of meeting. There is now another generation of ten-years-olds from those same communities dreaming that we would drop by and touch their hands. The deplorable conditions in our communities forbid us from becoming another elite group of *"untouchables,"* people who are cold, distant, and far removed from the children who have lost their ability to dream. Neither can we afford to be a status-conscience group who has forgotten how it feels to be poor, or how it was to take hammers and nails and needles and thread to make the best of whatever we had.

The true purpose of this book is to help us remember the rights and wrongs, the pains and the problems, the sorrows and the solutions that were part of our past... a past that forced us to depend on God and on each other because there were no government programs... a past when we were not mere neighbors, but a family with a common goal and a common cause: to build healthy children and peaceful communities.

I pray that we will become a family again. I pray that we will be more committed to each other than to political affiliations. Like Booker T. Washington, I pray that those who have been blessed with success will one day, feel the joy of not merely giving money and speeches, but of coming back home each year and physically giving of themselves so that those who are left behind will know that we really care.

Our Closing Prayer

"God of our weary years,
God of our silent tears
Thou who hast brought us thus far on the way,
Thou who hast by Thy might
Led us into the light,
Keep us forever in the path, we pray.
Lest our feet, stray from the places, our God, where we met Thee,
Lest our hearts, drunk with the wine of the world, we forget Thee;
Shadowed beneath Thy hand,
May we forever stand,
True to our God,
True to our native land."

Benediction
Psalms 67

God be merciful unto us, and bless us; and cause your face to shine upon us, that thy way may be known upon earth, and thy saving health among all nations. Let the people praise thee, O God; let all the people praise thee. Then shall the earth yield her increase, and God, even our own God, shall **bless us**.

Footnotes

Footnotes

Introduction

[1] John Hope Franklin, *Black Americans* (New York: Time Life Books, 1973), p. 19.

[2] Allen W. Trelease, *Reconstruction: The Great Experience* (New York: Harper & Row Publisher, 1971), p. 226.

[3] John Hope Franklin, *Reconstruction After The Civil War* (New York: McGraw Hill), p. 157.

[4] Herbert Aptheker, *Documentary History of Negro People in the United States Vol. 2* (New York: Carol Publishers, 1990), pp. 741-742.

[5] James M. McPherson, *The Abolitionist Legacy From Reconstruction To NAACP* (New Jersey: Princeton University 1975), p. 160.

Chapter One

[6] Nancy Boyd-Franklin, *Black Families In Therapy* (New York: The Guilford Press, 1989), p. 79.

[7] Jan Gleiter and Kathleen Thompson, *Biographical Stories: Booker T. Washington* (Austin Texas: Raintree Publishers, 1988), pp. 1-32.

[8] Rackham Holt, *George Washington Carver: An American Biography* (Garden City, New York: Doubleday, 1944), p. 25.

[9] Holt, pp. 250-253.

[10] William J. Federer, *America's God and Country Encyclopedia of Quotations* (St Louis, MO: AmeriSearch, 1994), p. 94.

[11] Darlene Clarke Hine, *Black Women in America* (Brooklyn, New York: Carlson Publishing, 1993), p. 1175.

[12] Hine, p. 1179.

[13] Federer, p. 592.

[14] Herbert Aptheker, *Documentary History of Negro People in the United States Vol. 1* (New York: Carol Publishers, 1951), pp. 267-273.

[15] Federer, p. 220.

[16] Herbert Aptheker, *Vol. 1*, p. 122.

[17] Herbert Aptheker, *Vol. 1*, pp. 24-25.

[18] Dennis P. Eichorn, *Cosby* (Seattle, WA: Turman Publishing Co., 1986), p. 9.
[19] Franklin, *Black Americans*, p. 40.
[20] Franklin, *Black Americans*, p. 86.
[21] Boyd-Franklin, p. 81.
[22] Boyd-Franklin, p. 81.

Chapter Two

[23] "Interview with Dr. King," *Playboy,* January 1965.
[24] "Lost Tribes Lost Knowledge," *Time Magazine,* September 1991.
[25] Arthur Schlesinger, *Disuniting of America* (New York: W. W. Norton Co. 1991), p. 5.
[26] Hayim Halevy Donin, *To Raise a Jewish Child* (1977), pp. 8-9.
[27] Sarah Silberstein Swartz, *Bar Mitzvah* (Garden City, New York: Doubleday, 1985), p. 2.
[28] "The Black Church," *Christianity Today*, March 1996.
[29] Encyclopedia Britannica Macropedia, "Slavery" (Chicago IL: 1992), Vol. 27, p. 287.
[30] "The Black Church," *Christianity Today*, March 1996.
[31] "The Black Church," *Christianity Today,* March 1996.
[32] Bruce Chadwick, *When the Game Was Black & White* (New York: Abberville Press), pp. 165-170.

Chapter Three

[33] "Revisiting Mt. Carmel Through Charitable Choice," *Christianity Today,* June 11, 2001.
[34] "God vs Gangs," *Newsweek,* June 1, 1998.
[35] Floyd Flake, *The Way of Bootstrapper* (San Francisco: Harper, 2000), p. 199.

Chapter Four

[36] Franklin, *Black Americans*, p. 109.
[37] Franklin, *Black Americans*, pp. 109-111.

[38] David Herbert Donald, *Charles Sumner* (New York: DA Capo, 1996), pp. 297-298.

[39] James M. McPherson, *Struggles for Equality* (Princeton, New Jersey: Princeton University Press, 1964), p. 23.

[40] Malcom Charles Moos, *The Republicans: A History of Their Party* (New York: Random House, 1956), p. 72.

[41] "The Prayer of Twenty Million," *New York Tribune* August 22, 1862

[42] McPherson, *Struggles for Equality*, p. xi.

[43] Kenneth M. Stampp, *Causes of the Civil War* (New York: Simon & Schuster, 1991), p. 141.

[44] John Hope Franklin and Alfred A. Moss, Jr., *From Slavery To Freedom* (New York: McGraw Hill 1988), pp. 226-234.

[45] Aptheker, *Vol. 2*, p. 579.

[46] Aptheker, *Vol. 2*, p. 739.

[47] Aptheker, *Vol. 2*, pp. 594-599.

[48] Aptheker, *Vol. 2*, pp. 600-604.

[49] McPherson, *The Abolitionist Legacy From Reconstruction To NAACP*, p. 40.

[50] Aptheker, *Vol. 2*, pp. 799-803.

[51] Franklin, *Black Americans*, p. 59.

[52] Franklin, *Black Americans*, p. 59.

[53] Stampp, p. 136.

Chapter Five

[54] "Getting Ready To Die Young," *Washington Post Newspaper* November 1, 1993.

[55] "Most Federal Firing Are Minority," *Knight Ridder Newspaper* December 14, 1993.

[56] "Interviews with Presidential Candidates Al Gore & George Bush," *Ebony,* 2002.

[57] "We've Beem Bill-boozled," *Savoy,* May 2001.

[58] Martin Luther King, Jr., *Why We Can't Wait* (New York: New American Library, 2000), pp. 6-7.

[59] Harry A. Ploski and James Williams, *The Negro Almanac: A Reference Work on the African American Fifth Edition* (Detroit: Gale Research, 1989), 377.

Chapter Six

[60] "The Congressional Black Caucus," *Savoy,* May 2001.

[61] Tony Brown, *Black Lies, White Lies* (New York: Quill William Morrow, 1995), pp. 235-246.

[62] "Civil Rights Groups Out of Step," *USA Today* February 24, 1992.

[63] "The Leadership of Black America," *The Economist Magazine* August 18, 2001, pp. 21-22.

[64] Brown, p. 235.

[65] Aptheker, *Vol. 2*, pp. 770-771.

[66] U.S. District Federal Court Charles Fairchild v Department of Labor Case #CV92-5765 Kn.

[67] U.S. Department of Commerce, Department of Commerce Bureau of Labor & Statistical Abstract 1986 & 2000 : Unemployment Statistics.

[68] "Do Black Americans Still Need Black Leadership," *Wall Street Journal,* April 18, 2001.

[69] "If Dr. King Were Alive," *Ebony,* January 1993, pp. 114-116.

[70] Flake, p. 199.

Chapter Seven

[71] Encyclopedia Britannica, Vol. 9 "Reconstruction" (Chicago IL: 1992), p. 979.

[72] Trelease, pp. 162-165.

[73] Franklin and Moss, pp. 226-233.

[74] Franklin, *Reconstruction After the Civil War*, p. 157.

[75] McPherson, *The Abolitionist Legacy From Reconstruction To NAACP*, p. 40.

[76] Donald, p. 420.

[77] Howard O. Lindsey, *History of Black America* (New Jersey: Chartwell Books, 1994), pp. 88-89.

[78] David L. Cohn, *The Fabulous Democrats* (New York: Putman, 1956), pp. 29-73.

[79] Stampp, pp. 146-147.

[80] Brown, p. 235.

[81] Ploski and Williams, pp. 609-610.

Chapter Eight

[82] McPherson, *The Struggle of Equality*, p. xi.

[83] Federer, p. 77.

[84] McPherson, *The Abolitionist Legacy From Reconstruction To NAACP*, pp. 174-175.

[85] Franklin, *Black Americans*, p. 95.

[86] Ploski and Williams, p. 260.

[87] McPherson, *The Abolitionist Legacy From Reconstruction To NAACP*, pp. 154-159.

Chapter Nine

[88] Aptheker, *Vol. 2*, p. 770.

[89] "William Raspberry Interview," *Newsweek*, April 6, 1992.

[90] King, Afterword.

Chapter Ten

[91] "The Black Church," *Christianity Today*, March 1996, pp. 36-30.

[92] "The Black Church," *Christianity Today,* March 1996.

[93] Aptheker, *Vol 2*, p. 661.

[94] "Interview With Dr. King," *Playboy*, January 1965.

Appendices

Appendix A

The Presidents of The United States

President	Date	Party
Thomas Jefferson	1801-1809	Democrat/Republican
James Madison	1809-1817	Democrat/Republican
James Monroe	1817-1825	Democrat/Republican
John Quincy Adams	1825-1829	Democrat/Republican
Andrew Jackson	1829-1837	Democrat
Martin Van Buren	1837-1841	Democrat
William H. Harrison	1841	Whig
John Tyler	1841-1845	Democrat/Whig
James K. Polk	1845-1849	Democrat
Zachary Taylor	1849-1850	Whig
Millard Fillmore	1850-1853	Whig
Franklin Pierce	1853-1857	Democrat
James Buchanan	1857-1861	Democrat
Abraham Lincoln	1861-1865	**Republican**
Andrew Johnson	1865-1869	**Republican**
Ulysses S. Grant	1869-1877	**Republican**
Rutherford B. Hayes	1877-1881	**Republican**
James A. Garfield	1881	**Republican**

Chester Alan Arthur	1881-1885	**Republican**
Grover Cleveland	1885-1889	Democrat
Benjamin Harrison	1889-1893	**Republican**
Grover Cleveland	1893-1897	Democrat
William McKinley	1897-1901	**Republican**
Theodore Roosevelt	1901-1909	**Republican**
William Howard Taft	1909-1913	**Republican**
Woodrow Wilson	1913-1921	Democrat
Warren G. Harding	1921-1923	**Republican**
Calvin Coolidge	1923-1929	**Republican**
Herbert Hoover	1929-1933	**Republican**
Franklin D. Roosevelt	1933-1945	Democrat
Harry S. Truman	1945-1953	Democrat
Dwight D. Eisenhower	1953-1961	**Republican**

Appendix B

One Year of Southern Lynching for the Year 1900

Name	Date	State
Henry Giveney Ripley	January 9th	Tennessee
Roger Giveney Ripley	January 9th	Tennessee
Walter Cotton	March 24th	Virginia
Williams Edward	March 27th	Mississippi
Moses York	April 16	Mississippi
Marshall Jones	May 4th	Georgia
Alexander Whitney	May 13th	Georgia
William Willis	May 14th	Georgia
Name Unknown	May 14th	Florida
Name Unknown	May 14th	Florida
Name Unknown	June 10th	Florida
Nate Mullins	June 17th	Arkansas
Robert Davis	June 21st	Florida
John Jennings	July 12th	Georgia
Robert Charles	July 26th	Louisiana
Name Unknown	September 11th	N. Carolina
Thomas J. Amos	September 11th	Louisiana
Frank Brown	September 7th	Mississippi
David Moore	September 14th	Mississippi

Name	Date	State
William Brown	September 14th	Mississippi
Wiley Johnson	October 9th	Louisiana
Gloster Barnes	October 23rd	Mississippi
Name Unknown	December 19th	Mississippi
Mr. Lewis	December 20th	Mississippi
John Hughley	April 22nd	Florida
S.A. Jenkins	June 17th	Arkansas
W.W. Watts	June 5th	Virginia
George Ratliffe	March 4th	N. Carolina
Thomas Clayton	March 10th	Mississippi
Allen Brooks	April 3rd	Georgia
John Peters	April 20th	West Virginia
Name Unknown	May 7th	Alabama
Dago Pete	June 3rd	Mississippi
Frank Gilmore	June 23rd	Louisiana
Elijah Clark	July 23rd	Alabama
Jack Hillsman	July 24th	Georgia
Jack Betts	August 13th	Mississippi
Name Unknown	August 19th	Virginia
Name Unknown	August 26th	Tennessee
Frank Hardenman	October 19th	Georgia

Name	Date	State
Daniel Long	December 8th	Virginia
Name Unknown	December 21st	Arkansas
John Bailey	March 18th	Georgia
Charles Humphries	March 18th	Alabama
Henry McAfee	April 19th	Mississippi
William Lee	May 11th	West Virginia
Henry Harris	May 15th	Louisiana
Simon Adams	June 9th	Georgia
Senny Jefferson	June 11th	Georgia
Jack Thomas	June 27th	Florida
John Roe	July 6th	Alabama
Logan Reoms	September 10th	Tennessee
Winfield Thomas	October 2nd	Alabama
Fratur Warfield	October 18th	Kentucky
Name Unknown	July 25th	Louisiana
August Thomas	July 25th	Louisiana
Baptiste Filean	July 25th	Louisiana
Louis Taylor	July 25th	Louisiana
Anna Marbry	July 25th	Louisiana
Name Unknown	July 25th	Louisiana
Silas Jackson	July 25th	Louisiana

Name	Date	State
James Suer	October 24th	Georgia
James Calaway	October 24th	Georgia
Luis Rice Ripley	March 23rd	Tennessee
Henry Ratcliff	May 1st	Mississippi
George Gordon	May 1st	Mississippi
Grant Weley	September 8th	Georgia
Mr. Askew	June 10th	Mississippi
Mr. Reese	June 10th	Mississippi
John Sanders	June 10th	Florida
Jordan Hines	June 27th	Georgia
James Barco	June 20th	Florida
Name Unknown	May 7th	Mississippi
Name Unknown	April 5th	Virginia
George Faller	December 28th	Georgia
Rufus Salter	January 11th	S. Carolina
Anderson Gause	January 16th	Tennessee
Jefferson Henry	July 9th	Louisiana
James Crosby	March 4th	Alabama
Seth Cobb	June 12th	Louisiana
George Ritter	March 22nd	N. Carolina
Name Unknown	May 26th	Arkansas

Name	Date	State
Mr. Williams	October 8th	Tennessee
George Beckham	September 21st	Louisiana
Charles Elliott	September 21st	Louisiana
Nathaniel Bowman	September 21st	Louisiana
Isaiah Rollins	September 21st	Louisiana
John Brodie	June 12th	Arkansas
Name Unknown	November 15th	Texas
Name Unknown	November 15th	Texas
Name Unknown	November 15th	Texas
William Burts	February 17th	S. Carolina
Samuel Hinson	May 16th	Mississippi
Mr. Abernathy	October 30th	Alabama

Appendix C

Terrorist Attacks by Democrats

and Their Klan Supporters

October 1869	Mob shoots Mr. Shepherd near Parksville.
November 1869	Klan shoots man at Frank Searcy's house in Madison County.
November 1869	Mob hangs Mr. Searcy in Richmond.
November 1869	Klan shoots Robert Mershon's daughter.
November 1869	Mob whips Pope Hall in Willett Washington County
December 1869	Mob takes two Negroes from jail and hangs one.
December 1869	Mob kills two Negroes while in custody near Mayfield.
December 24, 1869	Klan kills Allen Cooper in Adair County.
December 1869	Negro is whipped while on Scott's farm in Franklin County.
January 20, 1870	Mob hangs Charles Field in Fayette County.
January 31, 1870	Mob takes two men from Springfield jail and hangs them.
February 1870	Klan whips two Negroes in Madison County.

February 1870	Mob hangs Mr. Simms near Kingston Madison County.
February 1870	Mob hangs up Douglass Rodes and whipped him.
February 18, 1870	Mob hangs R.L. Byrom at Richmond.
April 5, 1870	Mob hangs Mr. Perry near Lancaster Garrad County.
April 6, 1870	Mob hangs Negro at Crab-Orchard in Lincoln County.
April 1870	Mob attacks Mr. Owen's home and shoots and kills Mr. Saunders.
April 11, 1870	Mob shoots and hangs Mr. Sam Lambert in Mercer County.
April 11, 1870	Mob releases five white prisoners from Federal officers.
April 1870	Mob kills William Hart at Mr. Palmer's house.
May 1870	Mob hangs three men near Gloscow Warren County.
May 1870	Ku Klux Klan kills John Reman in Adair County.
May 14, 1870	Mob hangs Mr. Pleasanton and Daniel and Willis Parker.
May 14, 1870	Ku Klux Klan robs Negroes and harasses them.
May 1870	Negro schoolhouse is burned by incendiaries in Christian County.

May 1870	Mob hangs Negro at Greenville Muhlenburgh.
June 4, 1870	Mob burns colored schoolhouse in Woodford County.
June 1870	Mob attacks jail and kills two men in Whitley County.
August 4, 1870	Riots occur during elections in Harrodsburg; four persons are killed.
August 10, 1870	Mob kills Turpin and Parker at Versilled.
August 1870	Band of men kills Simpson Grubbs in Montgomery County.
September 1870	Mob hangs Frank Timberlake at Flemingburg.
September 1870	Klan shoots and kills John Simes and his wife in Hay County.
September 1870	Klan hangs Oliver Williams in Madison County.
October 9, 1870	Klan shoots Howard Gilbert in Madison County.
October 1870	Klan drives colored people out of Bald-Knob Franklin County.
December 6, 1870	Two Negroes are shot on Harrison Blaton's farm near Frankfort.
December 18, 1870	Two Negroes are killed while in civil custody.
December 1870	Klan murders Howard Million in Fayette County.

December 12, 1870	John Dickerson is driven from home while his daughter is raped.
January 7, 1871	Mob hangs Negro named George at Cynthiana Harrison County.
January 7, 1871	Klan kills Negro near Ashland in Fayette County.
January 17, 1871	Mr. Hall is whipped and shot near in Shelby County.
January 14, 1871	Klan kills Negro in Hay County.
January 13, 1871	Negro Church and schoolhouse are burned in Scott County.

(Source: National Archives Washington, D.C. Records of U.S. Senate 42nd Congress first Session).

Appendix D

Unemployment Figures From 1965 To 2001

The following information was taken from Dept of Commerce's Statistical Abstract.

1965 Whites Unemployed 4.3% Blacks 8.5%   Gap 4.2%

1970 Whites Unemployed 3.9% Blacks 6.7%   Gap 2.8%

1975 Whites Unemployed 8.5% Blacks 14.7%   Gap 6.2%

1978 Whites Unemployed 5.8% Blacks 13.2%   Gap 7.4%

1979 Whites Unemployed 5.4% Blacks 12.6%   Gap 7.2%

1980 Whites Unemployed 6.0% Blacks 13.4%   Gap 7.4%

1981 Whites Unemployed 7.0% Blacks 15.9%   Gap 8.9%

1982 Whites Unemployed 8.6% Blacks 18.9%   Gap 10.3%

1983 Whites Unemployed 9.7% Blacks 21%   Gap 11.3%

1984 Whites Unemployed 7.2% Blacks 17.1%   Gap 9.9%

1985 Whites Unemployed 6.2% Blacks 15.1%   Gap 9.9%

1989 Whites Unemployed 4.5% Blacks 11.4%   Gap 6.9%

1990 Whites Unemployed 4.7% Blacks 11.3%   Gap 6.6%

1991 Whites Unemployed 6.0% Blacks 12.4%   Gap 6.4%

1992 Whites Unemployed 6.5% Blacks 14.1%   Gap 7.6%

1993 Whites Unemployed 6.0% Blacks 12.9%   Gap 6.9%

1994 Whites Unemployed 5.3% Blacks 11.5%   Gap 6.2%

1995 Whites Unemployed 4.9% Blacks 10.4%   Gap 5.5%

1996 Whites Unemployed 4.7% Blacks 10.5%   Gap 5.8%

1997 Whites Unemployed 4.2% Blacks 10.0%   Gap 5.8%

1998 Whites Unemployed 3.9% Blacks 8.9%   Gap 5.0%

1999 Whites Unemployed 3.7% Blacks 8.0%   Gap 4.3%

2000 Whites Unemployed 5.3% Blacks 10.8%   Gap 5.5%

2001 Whites Unemployed 6.5% Blacks 12.6%   Gap 6.1%

<u>Unemployment Among Teens Ages 16-19</u>

1994   Whites Unemployed 15.1%   Blacks 35.2%   Gap 20.1%

1995   Whites Unemployed 14.5%   Blacks 35.7%   Gap 21.2%

1996   Whites Unemployed 14.2%   Blacks 33.6%   Gap 19.4%

1997   Whites Unemployed 10.6%   Blacks 32.4%   Gap 21.8%

1998   Whites Unemployed 12.6%   Blacks 27.6%   Gap 15.0%

1999   Whites Unemployed 12.0%   Blacks 27.9%   Gap 15.9%

2000   Whites Unemployed 11.4%   Blacks 24.7%   Gap 13.3%

Note: Experts agree that the decline in black unemployment during 1998 and 1999 was not due to special programs specifically designed by the Congressional Black Caucus and the Clinton administration to reduce unemployment among Blacks. They believe blacks became the benefactors of a booming economy, much like those who benefited from Roosevelt's New Deal program of the 40's, which according to John Hope Franklin, was designed to reach the masses, not the blacks.

Appendix E

Black Members of Congress From 1870-1973

Black U.S. Senators

Name	Party	State	Date
Hiram R. Revel	Repub.	MS	1870-1871
Blanche K. Bruce	Repub.	MS	1875-1881
Edward Brooke	Repub.	MA	1967-1979

Black U.S. House of Representatives

Name	Party	State	Date
Joseph H. Rainey	Repub.	SC	1870-1879
Jefferson F. Long	Repub.	GA	1870-1871
Robert B. Elliott	Repub.	SC	1871-1874
Robert C. DeLarge	Repub.	SC	1871-1873
Benjamin S. Turner	Repub.	AL	1871-1873
Josiah T. Walls	Repub.	FL	1871-1873
Richard H. Cane	Repub.	SC	1873-1875+
John R. Lynch	Repub.	MS	1873-1877+
James T. Rapier	Repub.	AL	1873-1875
Alonzo J. Ransier	Repub.	SC	1873-1875
Jeremiah Haralson	Repub.	AL	1875-1877
John A, Hyman	Repub.	NC	1875-1877
Charles E. Nash	Repub.	LA	1875-1877
Robert Smalls	Repub.	SC	1875-1879
James E. O'Hara	Repub.	NC	1883-1887
Henry P. Cheatharn	Repub.	NC	1889-1893
John M. Langston	Repub.	VA	1890-1891
Thomas E. Miller	Repub.	SC	1890-1891
George W. Murray	Repub.	SC	1893-1895+
George W. White	Repub.	NC	1897-1901

(When Klan Terrorist Attacks Increased in the 1900s, Blacks Elected in South Decreased)

Name	Party	State	Date
Oscar DePreist	Repub.	IL	1929-1935
Arthur W. Mitchell	Dem.	IL	1935-1943
William L. Dawson	Dem.	IL	1943-1970
Adam C. Powell Jr.	Dem.	NY	1945-1967+
Charles C. Diggs Jr.	Dem.	MI	1955-1980
Robert N.C. Nix	Dem.	PA	1958-1978
Augustus F. Hawkins	Dem.	CA	1963-1973+
John Conyers Jr.	Dem.	MI	1965-1973+
William L. Clay	Dem.	MO	1969-1973+
Louis Stokes	Dem.	OH	1969-1973+
Shirley Chisholm	Dem	NY	1969-1982
George W. Collins	Dem	IL	1970-1972
Ronald V. Dellums	Dem.	CA	1971-1978
Ralph H. Metcalfe	Dem.	IL	1971-1978
Parren H. Mitchell	Dem.	MD	1971-1973+
Charles B. Rangel	Dem.	NY	1971-1973+
Walter E. Fauntroy	Dem	D.C.	1971-1973+
Yvorme B. Burke	Dem.	CA	1973+
Cardiss Collins	Dem.	CA	1973+
Barbara Jordan	Dem	TX	1973-1979

(Source: *The Negro Almanac*, p. 413)

Miss Jordan was the first Democrat ever to be elected to Congress from the South, almost 10 years after the passage of the 1964 Civil Right Act. Only six blacks were members of Congress when the 1964 Act was passed. Elected black officials were elected in areas where there were large black populations. Experts believe that it was the populated district of black voters, not the candidate's party affiliation that attributed to their success.

+ Represents additional years served beyond the date indicated.

Appendix F
Presidents' Appointments of Black Judges
(From Roosevelt To Reagan)

President	Party	Total Appointed		Blacks Appointed	
Franklin D. Roosevelt	Dem.	224 Judges	2		.89%
Harry S. Truman	Dem.	160 Judges	3		1.8%
Dwight D. Eisenhower	Repub.	180 Judges	2		1.1%
John F. Kennedy	Dem.	131 Judges	3		2.2%
Lyndon B. Johnson	Dem.	178 Judges	11		6.1%
Richard M. Nixon	Repub.	231 Judges	7		3.0%
Gerald Ford	Repub.	62 Judges	4		6.4%
Jimmy E. Carter	Dem.	259 Judges	38		14.6%
Ronald Reagan	Repub.	343 Judges	7		2.0%
Total		1,768 Judges	77		4.0%

(Source: *The Negro Almanac,* pp. 339-340)

These stats are not very impressive for either Democrats or Republicans.

Appendix G

Brief Chronology of Events Affecting

African Americans

1619   A Dutch ship delivered twenty blacks to the settlement in Jamestown, Virginia.

1700   Slave population reached 28,000 in the U.S. with 23,000 located in the South.

1776   On July 4, 1776, 57 men signed America's first important document, The Declaration of Independence. The Declaration declared that, *"that all men are created equal."* Besides the use of Scripture (such as Luke 4:18), this portion of the Declaration became the Abolitionist's primary argument in their quest to abolish slavery. Using Genesis 9:25, slave owners countered and said the statement does not apply to African Americans who were cursed by God and condemned to perpetual servitude. The debate would continue through the Democrat's victory in Dred Scott decision and the Republican's victory with the passage of the 13th, 14th and 15th Amendments. The issue of equality was finally adjudicated 178 years later with the 1954 Brown vs Board of Education decision, a decision that Democrats were strongly opposed to.

1787   The Constitution was signed by 38 members of the Constitutional Convention. Article 1 of the Constitution gave each state the right to have representatives in Congress. The Article stated that the number of congressional representatives from each state would be determined by the total number of persons residing in those states. After much debate, the Constitutional Convention gave slaves states authorization to classify each slave as three-fifth of a person - for the sole purpose of increasing the southern population. African Americans were not only used as free labor. Their three-fifth classification was also used to increase the southern population so southern slave-owners could gain and maintain control of Congress.

1791   Four years later, Congress added 10 Amendments to the Constitution (also known as the Bill of Rights). The First Amendment, which states: *"Congress shall make no law respecting an establishment of religion or prohibiting the free exercise thereof."* gave freed blacks the right to establish their own churches and denominations (See Rev. Richard Allen 1794).

This Amendment also backed up Congress' earlier rulings when they approved a request from a magazine publisher (Robert Aitken) to print Bibles for the public schools. Aitken's request was made on January 21, 1781. Congress approved his request on September 10, 1782 and stipulated that each Bible printed must include the following statement: *"The United States Congress recommends this Bible for the inhabitants of the United States."* Five years earlier, in 1777 and one year after the Declaration of Independence was signed, Congress was concerned that there weren't enough Bibles in the United States and issued an order to import an additional 20,000 Bibles from *"Holland, Scotland and elsewhere."*

Source: Myth of Separation 1992, p. 104, p. 106, Journals of Continental Congress Vol. VIII, 1777, p. 734, Journals of Continental Congress, Vol. XXIII, 1782, p.574, American God & Country Encyclopedia of Quotations, 1996, p. 324, J.O Wilson Public Schools of Washington D.C. - Historical Society Vol. 5, p. 5.

1794   Rev. Richard Allen, a slave who purchased his own freedom, became the first African American pastor in America. On July 17, 1794, Allen exercised his constitutional right and opened the Bethel Church of Philadelphia, the first African American church in America.

1801   During slavery, the Bible (with few exceptions) was the only book that slaves were permitted to read. Slaves weren't the only ones who were encouraged to the read the Bible. In 1801, ten years after adding the Amendment which states: ***"Congress shall make no law respecting an establishment of religion or prohibiting the free exercise thereof,"*** the Bible took center stage again.

President Thomas Jefferson, a former slave owner (who also served as the Chairman of the District of Columbia School District at that time) - developed a new plan for educating students. The plan approved the use of Bibles and Isaac Watts' Psalms, Hymns, and Spiritual songs as the principal books for teaching students how to read.

1802   A year after President Thomas Jefferson adopted the Bible as the primary reading book for public schools in the District of Columbia, he shared his thoughts about the relationship between government and religion in a January 1, 1802 letter to the Danbury Baptist Association (of Danbury, Connecticut). The Baptist Association had written the President because they had heard rumors that Congress was considering a bill to establish a national Christian denomination. In Jefferson's response, he stated that Congress was not and could not pass a law to establish a national Christian denomination, because he believed there was a *"wall of separation between church and state."*

Even though Jefferson had approved the use of the Bible for the District of Columbia School District a year earlier, he did not feel that his actions **violated of the First Amendment** or a violated what he referred to as the *"separation between church and state."* His decision to use the Bible was a school district decision, it was not the results of *Congress making a law to establish a religion.* The Bible's universal appeal and acceptance had a profound impact on African Americans. For African Americans, the Bible became the Constitution of their culture and the black Christian minister became the captain of their communities. During Reconstruction, nearly all of the black politicians came from the ranks of the black clergy and all were Republican.

1820   The Missouri Compromise was reached. Missouri became a slave state and Maine became a free state. Twelve states were free and twelve were slave.

1831   Abolitionist William Garrison founded *The Liberator*, a newspaper that focused on the issues of slavery.

1831   Nat Turner led a violent slave rebellion in Southampton, Virginia. Sixty whites were killed. On October 30th, Nat was captured; twelve days later he was hung.

1833   Philadelphia organized the first American Antislavery Society.

1834   British abolished slavery; 700,000 slaves were freed.

1847   Dred Scott filed a lawsuit in St. Louis for his freedom, claiming that his master had taken him to live in Minnesota, a state that did not allow slavery.

1852   Harriet Beecher Stowe's book, *Uncle Tom's Cabin*, was released and the horrors of slavery were revealed.

1854   Stephen Douglas successfully pushed through the Kansas-Nebraska Act, allowing both states to enter the Union without any restrictions forbidding slavery. This violated the Missouri Compromise.

1854   The Republican Party was started (originally formed in Jackson, Michigan). The party's founders were firmly linked in common opposition to slavery and more particularly, to the recent passage of the Kansas-Nebraska Act (which extended slavery into the new territories).

1856   Republicans had their first National Convention. They adopted a platform that stated Congress did not have the right to recognize slavery, but should have an obligation and a right to abolish slavery.

1856   Pro-slavery forces (Democrat supporters) invaded Lawrence, Kansas, an integrated abolitionist town. Several people were killed and several buildings were burned.

1856   While Republican Senator Charles Sumner of Massachusetts gave a fiery speech opposing slavery and the killings in Lawrence, Kansas, he was attacked and nearly beaten to death by Democratic Congressman Preston S. Brooks of South Carolina. A violent fistfight ensued between Democrats and Republicans when Republicans came to Sumner's rescue.

1856   Nine years after Dred Scott filed his lawsuit, a Supreme Court controlled by Southern Democrats finally heard the Dred Scott Case. The court upheld the lower court's ruling. In its opinion, the court said the Constitution protected the rights of citizens to own property and that slaves were considered property, not citizens of the United States (according to the Constitution and the Declaration of Independence). Chief Justice Taney delivered the opinion. Taney said that the Constitution protects private property and it makes no distinction between the various types of property owned by it citizens.

1858   The debate between Lincoln and Douglas heated up the controversy over slavery.

1858   Using the Dred Scott decision as a basis, the U.S. Attorney ruled that slaves could not patent inventions because they weren't citizens of the United States.

1859   John Brown and his band of thirteen whites and five blacks fought pro-slavery forces at Harper's Ferry, Virginia. Two blacks were killed, two escaped, and one was captured.

1860   The divide between the Democrats and the Republican widened as they both took firm positions on the issue of slavery. One party supported it, the other party opposed it. On December 17, 1860, South Carolina secedes from the Union.

1860   Lincoln was elected as the first Republican President of the United States on an anti-slavery platform.

1861   Fort Sumter of South Carolina, which was occupied by federal troops, was attacked by Confederates. This marked the beginning of the Civil War.

1862   Congress approved the use of black soldiers in the Union army. During that same year, the Confederates captured a number of black soldiers and hung many.

1863   As the commander in chief of the U.S. Armed Forces, President Lincoln issued the Emancipation Proclamation effective January 1, 1863, freeing all slaves in the rebellious states (Southern slave-holding states).

1864   Lincoln is re-elected and this time his vice president is Andrew Johnson, a devout Democrat. Lincoln's former vice president Hannibal Hamlin, was a strong Republican who opposed slavery. Lincoln chose Johnson to broaden his base and to appeal to borderline Democrat.

1865   On April 9, 1865, Robert E. Lee and the Confederate army surrendered and the Civil War was ended. A total of 179,000 blacks served in the Union army. Three thousand were killed in battle and 26,000 died from diseases.

1865   Southern Democrats passed Black Codes to suppress, restrict, and deny blacks the same privileges granted to whites. The Codes forced blacks to serve as apprentices to their former slave masters.

1865   Republicans enacted the Freedmen Bureau to assist the newly freed slaves. The Freedman Bureau was designed to provide basic health and educational services for the freedmen and to oversee all land abandoned in the South during the war.

1865   Lincoln was assassinated by John Wilkes Booth on April 15, 1865, just six days after the war ended. Vice President Andrew Johnson (a Southern Democrat) was sworn in as the new president. President Johnson said, "This is a country for white men and long as I am president it will be a government for white men."

1865   On October 19, 1865, just six months after Lincoln's death, President Johnson ordered General Oliver O. Howard (a former Union officer) to travel to the South and have all Southern blacks return land to their former slave masters. The land was given to blacks during the war by Union officers when white slaver owners abandoned the land. General Howard, a devout Christian who strongly opposed slavery, was sadden when he was given the orders.

1865   December 18, 1865, a Republican administration signed into law the Thirteenth Amendment to outlaw slavery. It stated that neither slavery nor involuntary servitude shall exist in the United States or in any other place where it had jurisdiction, except for a punishment of crime when one has been duly convicted in the court of law. This amendment also said that Congress had the legislative powers to enforce this law.

1866   On March 3, 1866, the Republicans passed the Freedmen's Bureau Extension Act to strengthened their 1866 Freedmen's Program.

1866   On April 9, 1866, ten years after the Dred Scott Decision, Republicans passed the Civil Rights Act of 1866. The law provided blacks protection from the Black Codes and other repressive legislation initiated by Southern Democrats. The law declared that all citizens born in the United States and those not subject to any foreign power, (excluding Indians not taxed), are hereby declared to be citizens of the United States. It went on to say that such citizens of every race and color, without regard to any previous condition of slavery or involuntary servitude, shall have the same right in every Territory in the United States to make and enforce contracts, to sue, be parties, and give evidence, to inherit, purchase, lease, sell, hold and convey real and personal property and to full and equal benefit of all laws.

1866   The Ku Klux Klan was formed and became the terrorist arm of the Democrat Party. Their primary goal was to intimidate and terrorize black voters, Republicans, and any whites that supported them.

1866   Edward G. Walker and Charles L. Mitchell were the first blacks elected to serve in a legislative assembly in the United States. They were Republicans and were members of the House of Representatives in Massachusetts.

1867   The Republicans passed the First Reconstruction Act of 1867 to establish a new government system in the South, one that would be fair to blacks.

1867   Morehouse and Howard Universities were opened with the support of Republicans and abolitionists who were members of various missionary groups that founded and funded schools for blacks.

1868   On July 23, 1868, the Republicans ratified the Fourteenth Amendment to established that every citizen in the United States (including the former slaves) were citizens and that no state could deprive any person of life, liberty, or property without due process of the law; nor could they deny to any person within it jurisdiction the equal protection of laws.

1870   On March 30, 1870, the Republicans ratified the Fifteenth Amendment to establish the right to vote for all citizens.

1871   Republicans introduced the Ku Klux Klan Act to end intimidation and violence against blacks, whites, and Republicans who supported blacks.

1871   The U.S. Senate Joint Select Committee investigated complaints of voter harassment initiated by Southern Democrats and their Klan supporters.

1874   Many blacks moved to Kansas to escape the terror and the oppression of the Democrats and the Ku Klux Klan. Many blacks died en route to Kansas.

1875   Democrat supporters in the state of Tennessee passed Jim Crow Laws to restrict the rights of blacks to use public facilities.

1875   Republicans passed the Civil Rights Act of 1875 which prohibited racial discrimination in places of public accommodation.

1875   Blanche K. Bruce of Mississippi became the only black to serve a full term in the Senate until the middle of the twentieth century. Bruce was a Republican.

1876   President Grant sent federal troops to the South to protect
        black citizens shortly after five blacks were killed by Southern
        Democrats.

1877   Rutherford Hayes is elected after he promises to remove federal
        troops from the South. The federal troops were sent there to pro-
        tect black citizens after Senate investigations proved that many
        black voters were murdered and harassed by Democrats and their
        terrorist supporters. Hayes' action was referred to as the "Com-
        promise of 1877." This was the official end to Reconstruction.

1884   Former black Congressman John Roy Lynch is elected as the
        temporary chairman of the Republican Convention, the first black
        to preside over a national political convention.

1884   The Senate conducted more interviews with blacks on voter
        harassment by the Democrats and their Klan supporters.

1891   Lynching of blacks becomes a common occurrence, particularly
        in the Democratic-controlled South.

1896   The U.S. Supreme Court issues its ruling in the case of Plessy v
        Ferguson and established the "separate but equal" doctrine. The
        court opinion stated that it was not a violation of the Constitution
        to have separate facilities for blacks. Homer Plessy filed the suit
        after he was arrested for refusing to move to a section of the train
        that was reserved for blacks only.

1898   Democrats in Wilmington, North Carolina, launched a very
        vicious political campaign to get rid of all black Republican offi-
        cials. They threatened to kill blacks if they voted Republican and
        told white voters that black elected officials and business owners
        wanted to rape white women. To assure victory, Democrats stuffed
        ballot boxes. They celebrated their victory by killing blacks and
        running them out of town. The word spread throughout the South.
        More blacks were lynched and murdered. Blacks appealed to
        President McKinley and he turned a deaf ear to their cries. Sev-
        enty-five years passed before the South elected a black person to

Congress from either party. (In 1975 Barbara Jordan of Texas was elected).

1900   The lynching of blacks increased dramatically in the South.

1909   Three whites who opposed the lynching of blacks and the racist practices of the Democrats, founded the NAACP on President Lincoln's 100th birthday, February 12, 1909.

1912   During the Wilson administration, Congress, which was controlled by the Democrats, recieved the greatest number of bills proposing racial segregation and discrimination that had ever been introduced.

1930   Franklin D. Roosevelt receives the black vote by the endorsement of black newspapers and becomes the 32nd President of the United States. Shortly after taking office, Roosevelt banned the black newspaper from the military, claiming they were communist, and he refused to pass laws that would stop the Klan's activities.

1941   President Roosevelt signed Executive Order 8802 to end discriminatory practices in the defense industry.

1948   President Truman signed Executive Order 9981 to start the process to end segregation in the Arm Forces. The process was completed under President Eisenhower.

1957   Republicans fought to pass the Civil Rights Act of 1957 and the
&   Civil Rights of 1960 in a Democrat-controlled Congress. The
1960   laws were designed to create the Civil Rights Commission that Roosevelt and Truman refused to form. In addition to the Civil Rights Commission, the acts provided additional civil rights and voting rights protection. Southern Democrats opposed both laws. William Colmer, a Democratic Congressman from Mississippi, said the passage of the law would "curtail the freedom and the real rights of the citizens of all sections" and would "cause further regimentation of our citizens."

1962   With President John F. Kennedy's blessings, Democratic Attorney General, Robert Kennedy approved wiretaps on Dr. Martin Luther King Jr. in an attempt to prove that the Civil Right's leader was associated with the Communist Party. See the strained relationship between Dr. Martin Luther King and President John F. Kennedy in Appendix H's 1964 Civil Rights Act and Dr. King's statement on page 80.

1963   Democratic Attorney General, Robert Kennedy approved wire taps on Martin Luther King Jr. in an attempt to prove that the Civil Rights Movement was influenced by the Communist Party. See the strained relationship Dr. Martin Luther King had with President John F. Kennedy in Appendix H 1964 Civil Rights Act.

1964   Republicans provided the support needed to pass the 1964 Civil Rights Act. More Republicans voted for this law than Democrats. Because of the strong opposition by Southern Democrats, the debate on this bill lasted over eighty days, took up some 7,000 pages in the Congressional Record, and created the longest filibuster in Senate history. Over 10,000,000 words were devoted to the subject by members of the upper house. Just before the bill was signed Senator Richard Russell, a Democrat from Georgia and the leader of the southern anti-civil rights senators, said, *"The moving finger is writing the final act of the longest debate and the greatest tragedy ever played out in the Senate."*

1965   On March 15, 1965, President Lyndon Johnson spoke to the joint session of Congress and called for new legislation to secure the right to vote. When the Senate received the bill two days later, the debate **for** the bill began with words from Republican Senator Everett Dirksen from Illinois. During the debates, Democrats from the South focused on various literacy tests designed to disqualify Negro voters. Senator Herman Talmadge (Democrat from Georgia) and Sam Ervin (Democrat from North Carolina) characterized the bill as one *"tearing the Constitution asunder and one worthy of Hitler or Genghis Khan."* Despite their opposition, the Voting Rights Act of 1965 was passed.

1967   Angry with Dr. Martin Luther King's protest against the Viet Nam War, Democratic President, Lyndon B. Johnson referred to Dr. King as *"that Nigger preacher."*

1968   In reference to Dr. King leaving Memphis Tennessee after riots broke out in March of 1968 where a teenager was killed, Democratic Senator Robert Bryd, referred to Dr. King as a *trouble-maker* who starts trouble, but runs like a coward after trouble is ignited. A few weeks later, Dr. King returned to Memphis and was assassinated on April 4, 1968.

1968   On April 11, 1968, The Civil Rights Act of 1968 was passed with opposition from Southern Democrats. Again it was Republican Senator Everett Dirksen of Illinois who provided the proper language and changes to get this bill passed. The law prohibited discrimination in housing.

1972   Under President Richard Nixon (Republican), the Congress passed the 1972 Equal Employment Opportunity Act giving the Civil Rights Commission the authority to issue judicially enforceable cease and desist orders in cases involving discriminatory employment practices. This act also paved the way for Executive Order 11248 and affirmative action programs with quotas, goals, and timetables.

1972   Equal Opportunity Act of 1972 Revision which prohibited employment discrimination in the private sector, now included federal, state, and local government employers.

1973   The Comprehensive Employment and Training Act of 1973 was passed (again under a Republican Administration) to provide federal funding to employ and train unskilled minority workers in federally assisted programs.

1982   The Voting Rights Act of 1965 Amendment of 1982 was passed with **bipartisan** support. The law was Congress's response to the Supreme Court's ruling in the *City of Mobile v Bolden* case. The act prohibited any voting practice or procedure "imposed or applied by any state or political subdivision in a manner which results in a denial or abridgement of the rights of any citizen of the United States to vote on account of race or color."

1983   After many prominent Republicans Senators convinced President Ronald Reagan that he should support a bill to establish a national holiday to honor Dr. Martin Luther King, Republican President, Ronald Reagan, signed the bill into law (October 20, 1983). Republican Senator, Jesse Helms, who led the effort to defeat the bill, accused Dr. King of being a Marxist. In the Senate the bill passed by a vote of 78-22 and in the House it passed by a vote of 338 to 90. Republicans in both the House and Senate ignored Senator Helms' racist efforts and voted for the bill.

1983   The Civil Rights Commission Act of 1983 created a **bipartisan** commission with four members appointed by the president and two by the Senate and the House.

1988   Under President Ronald Reagan, the Federal Contract Compliance and Workforce Development Act of 1988 was passed. The law was designed to improve the effectiveness of the enforcement of nondiscrimination and affirmative action requirements in federal contracts and to create a fund to be used to establish educational and training programs for minorities and women.

1994   December 15, the Honorable Judge David V. Kenyon ordered the Clinton Administration to force 100 member-shipping companies of the Pacific Maritime Association to develop an Affirmative Action Plan to stop discrimination against African Americans, Hispanic and female longshore workers along the west coast. Clinton left office six years later and never forced the companies to develop such a plan (case number CV925765Kn).

1995   The Clinton Administration filed a Reverse Discrimination suit against Illinois State University on behalf of a group of white janitors, but refused to help Black, Hispanic and female longshore workers who were employed by Pacific Maritime Association in the Seattle Tacoma area. Despite a court order dealing with these shipping companies, the Clinton Administration refused to help the workers.

2001   Associated Press reported that in states largely controlled by Democrats, blacks that had at one time owned over 15 million acres of land, now own only 2.2 million. AP reporters said that many blacks lost their land through cheating, intimidation and even murder.

2002   On December 3, 2002 President Clinton spoke to the Democratic Leadership Council at New York State University. He suggested a plan for the Democrats to re-gain the White House. **None of his recommendations dealt with providing more Civil Rights protection for African Americans nor did they include improving the deplorable conditions in the African American community.** His only reference to Civil Rights dealt with Civil Rights for Gays and his only reference to re-building communities dealt with re-building communities in other countries under the Marshall Plan. His primary theme was reaching out to the white middle class voters.

2003   During the Democratic Presidential debates, held on September 9, 2003, the Rev. Al Sharpton revealed shocking truths about the Democratic Party and its relationship to African Americans. Rev. Sharpton said, *"When I look around this country and see double unemployment in black communities, where we see that we're four times more likely to go to jail for the same crime, and we cannot get some **Democrats** to deal with it. You know, the only thing I never got over in life is – I took a young lady to a dance when I was in high school and she left with somebody else. And that's what the **Democrats** have done to the black community. We helped take you to the dance and you leave with right-wingers...."*

2003   During that same debate Congressman Dick Gephart discussed what he thought was the true relationship between the Democratic Party and African Americans. When asked if he would choose an African American for a running mate if he won his Party's Primary, he said, *"I have a friend in St Louis that I served in Congress*

with. His name is Bill Clay. His son, Lacy Clay, is one of the deputy chairs of my campaign. Bill wrote a book called "Permanent Interest." He said African Americans don't have permanent friends, they just have permanent interest. I think he's right."
Gephart never answered the question as to whether or not he would choose an African American to be his running mate.

2004   On January 11, 2004, Democratic Presidential candidate Howard Dean admitted that during his tenure as governor of Vermont (over 10 years), he had never hired a black or a Hispanic for any of his cabinet positions.

2004   As of 2004, the Democratic Party, which is the oldest party in America and claims it has blacks' best interest in mind, is the only party that has never elected a black ***man*** to the United States Senate. The Republican Party, which is the younger political party, has elected three African American males to the United States Senate.

Appendix H

Arguments Some Democrats Made

Against Key Civil Rights Legislation

The Thirteenth Amendment

Purpose: Sponsored by Republican Senator Lyman Trumbull of Illinois to free all slaves and abolish slavery in the United States and its territories.

Democrat's Opposition: "During the debates on March 19, 1864, **Democratic Congressman Fernando** Wood of New York said the following: *"The proposed Amendment to abolish slavery in the states of the Union is unjust, a breach of good faith and utterly irreconcilable... It involves the extermination of all white men of the southern States, and the forfeiture of all the land and other property belonging to them. Negroes and military colonist will take the place of the race* [that will be] *blotted out of existence."*

Republican James Wilson opening remarks included the following statement: *"It was perfectly natural for the comparatively few men who held four million human being in bondage which put to shame all other kindred systems which ever cursed man for their mildness, not only to resort to cruel an despotic laws for aid in their diabolical act, but also to seek refuge in the anti-republican dogma that "the right to govern resides in a very small minority...." "Mr. Chairman we can cast our eyes upon no page of this nation's history whereon it is not written, "Slavery is incompatible with a free government." "We have tried to close our eyes against this constantly repeated and self-evident truth. We have tried to reason it away, to practice arts which should carry us around it, over it, or under it. We have failed to accomplish the*

desired results. As immutable as the laws of God stands the decla-
ration, "Slavery is incompatible with a free government".... **"No**
religion which recognizes God's eternal attribute of justice *and*
breathes that spirit of love which applies to all men the sublime
commandments, "whatsoever ye would that men should do unto
you, do ye even so to them," can ever be allowed free exercise
where slavery curses men and defies God. *No religious, denomi-*
nation can flourish or even be tolerated where slavery rules with
surrendering the choices jewels of its faith into keeping of that
infidel power which withhold the Bible from the poor...."

1865 Black Codes

In 1865, shortly after the war, southern Democrats legislated
Black Codes to suppress, restrict and deny blacks the same privileges granted to whites. The Codes established whom blacks could
or could not work for, the type of employment they could pursue,
in addition to establishing evening curfews and restrictive travel.
Many blacks were forced to work for their former slave masters
as apprentices.

1866 Civil Rights Acts

Purpose: Introduced by Senator Lyman Trumbull of Illinois,
the law was designed to challenge Black Codes by prohibiting discrimination on the basis of race and assuring that every citizen had
the same rights to contract, sue, purchase and dispose property;
and to *"bring action and give evidence and to equal benefit of all*
laws of the security of person and property."
Democrat's Opposition: Reverdy Johnson, a Democrat
from Maryland argued against the law. Johnson argued that under
this law, the black man would have the *"same right to enter into a*

contract of marriage with a white woman as a white man has."
Republican Senator William Fessenden of Maine responded: *"He
[the black man] has the same right to make a contract of marriage
with a white woman that a white man has with a black woman."*
The Democrat from Maryland went on to argue that the 1866 Civil
Rights Act could not apply to blacks because the, *"The Supreme
Court had already ruled in the Dred Scott case that a person of
African descent, whether born free or not whether free by birth or
free by after events, is not within the meaning of the Constitution
of the United States, a citizen."* **Willard Saulsbury, a Democrat**
from Delaware said *"I regard this bill as one of the most dangerous that was ever introduced into the Senate of the United States...."*
*During the last four or five years I have sat in this Chamber and
witnessed the introduction of bills into this body which I thought
obnoxious to many very grave and serious constitutional objec-
tion: but I never since I have been a member of the body seen a bill
so fraught with danger, so full of mischief, as the bill now under
consideration."*   Please note: those opposing this bill were northern Democrats. The debates started on January 29, 1866, the same
year that the Ku Klux Klan was organized. **Martin Thayer the
Republican from Pennsylvania** responded: *"Sir, this bill is the
just sequel to, and the proper completion of, the great measure of
national redress which opened the dungeon doors of four million
human beings. Without this, in my judgment, that great act of justice will be paralyzed and made useless. With this, it will have
practical effect, life, vigor, and enforcement...."*

*Sir, if it is competent for the new-formed Legislatures of the
rebel States to enact laws which oppress this large class of people
who are dependent for protection upon the United States Government, to retain them still in a state of real servitude; if it is practi-
cable for these Legislatures to pass laws and enforce laws* [Black
Codes] *which reduce this class of people to the condition of bond-
men; laws which prevent the enjoyment of the fundamental rights
of citizenship; laws which declare, for example, that they shall not
have the privilege of purchasing a home for themselves and their*

families; laws which impair their ability to make contracts for labor in such a manner as virtually to deprive them of the power of making such contracts, and which then declare them vagrants because they have no homes and because they have not employment; I say, if it is competent for these Legislatures to pass and enforce such laws, then I demand to know, of what practical value is the amendment abolishing slavery in the United States? ...For one, sir, I thought when I voted for the amendment to abolish slavery that I was aiding to give real freedom to the men who had so long been groaning in bondage. I did not suppose that I was offering them a mere paper guarantee."

In Response to Martin Thayer's comments, **Michael Kerr the Democrat** from Indiana said, *"...The Constitution of Indiana, adopted in 1851, forbids any Negro or mulatto to come into or settle in that State after the adoption of that Constitution and declares all contracts made with any Negro or mulatto coming into the State contrary to the provision of that Constitution shall be void.* This bill [1866 Civil Rights Act] *proposes to annul those constitutional provisions and all State laws passed to secure their execution.... I might go on and in this manner to illustrate the practical working of this extraordinary measure. But I have said enough to indicate the inherent viciousness of the bill. It takes a long and fearful step toward the complete obliteration of Sate authority and the reserved and original rights of the States...."*

Freedman Bureau Extension Act of 1866

Purpose: Sponsored by Republicans, the Freedman Bureau was first established in 1865 to provide basic health and educational services for the newly freed slaves and displaced whites.

Democrat's Opposition: The Democrats opposed the Freedman Bureau (particularly the portion that provided aid to blacks) and did so by passing Black Codes, during the same year the war ended (1865). Through the Black Codes blacks were discouraged from going to school and were forced to be dependent on their former slave masters for their living. From 1865 to 1900, several black schools and colleges were established by Abolitionists, many of whom, were members of the Radical wing of the Republican Party.

The First Reconstruction Act of 1867

Purpose: This (Republican) bill was designed to rebuild the south with a bias-free government system that would be more favorable to the newly freed slaves. The Act included the following:

"Whereas no legal State governments or adequate protection for life or property now exists in the Rebel States of Virginia, North Carolina, South Carolina, Georgia, Mississippi, Alabama, Louisiana, Florida, Texas, and Arkansas; and whereas it is necessary that peace and good order should be forced in the said States until loyal and Republican State governments can be established: Therefore:

Be it enacted That said rebel States shall be divided into military districts and made subject to military authority of the United States.... (2) That it shall be the duty of the President to assign to the command of each of said districts an officer of the army, not below the rank of brigadier-general, and to detail a sufficient military force to enable such officer to perform his duties and enforce his authority within the district to which he is assigned...."

Democrat's Opposition: The Democrats formed various terrorist organizations such as the Ku Klux Klan to defeat and undermind the Republican's reconstruction efforts. African American Professor, John Hope Franklin said, *" When Southern whites had almost complete charge of Reconstruction, a kind of **guerrilla warfare** was carried out against both blacks and whites who represented the Washington government in the South. It had looked as though the Civil War would break out anew as **Democrats** resorted*

to every possible device to overthrow the radicals [Republicans]."
Like many of the terrorists groups in Iraq today (2003), the
Democrat's terrorist of 1867 were determined to stay in power and
defeat the efforts to reconstruct the South. The obstacles that the
Republicans faced in 1867 are quite similar to the obstacles that
the Bush Administration faced in Iraq (in 2003).   In both situations, the Bush Administration in 2003 and the Republican Administration in 1867 did not properly plan for Reconstruction. At no
time did they anticipate terrorist attacks by the loyal members of
the Baath Party during Iraq's Reconstruction or the terrorist
attacks by the loyal members of the Democratic Party during the
South's Reconstruction. In reference to the 1867 Reconstruction,
Professor David Herbert Donald of Harvard said: *"Congress could*
*give the Negro the vote, but all over the South **the Ku Klux Klan***
***and other terrorist organizations systematically** intimidated the*
freedman, flogged or slaughtered their leaders, and drove whites
who worked with them into exile. Congress could require federal
troops to supervise the registration of voters, but Negroes were
***waylaid and butchered** on the road to the registration*
office."   Forty years after the Democrats successfully defeated
Reconstruction in 1867, **Senator Ben Tillman of South Carolina**
said, *"We reorganized the Democratic Party with one plank, and*
the only plank, namely, that this is a white man's country, and white
men must govern it."

The Fourteenth Amendment

The Purpose: Introduced by Republican Senator, John
Bingham of Ohio and Congressman Thaddeus Stevens of Pennsyl-
vania, the bill was drafted in conjunction to the Reconstruction
Act to make all slaves citizens.

Democrat's Opposition: During the two year debate (from June 16, 1866 to July 28, 1868), the Democrats argued that the Dred Scott decision by the U.S. Supreme Court had already determined that Blacks were merely property, not citizens, and that Congress had no right or power to overturn the court's decision with this bill. **Congressman Andrew Rogers from New Jersey** said the proposed Amendment was *"an attempt to in-graft upon the Constitution of the United States one of the most dangerous, most wicked, most intolerant, and most outrageous propositions ever introduced into this house. I have no fault to find with the colored race. I wish them well, and if I were in a State where they exist in large numbers I would vote to give them every right enjoyed by the white people –* **except the right of a Negro man to marry a white woman and the right to vote**. *God save the people of the South from degradation by which they would be obliged to go to the polls and vote side by side with the Negro!"*

The Fifteenth Amendments

The Purpose: Introduced by a Republican Senate, the purpose of this Amendment was to give Blacks the Constitutional right to vote.

Democrat Opposition: **Garrett Davis, Democratic Congressman from Kentucky** said, *"Sir, these amendments of the Constitution, your Freedmen's Bureau bill, your civil rights bill, and all of your monstrous and unconstitutional laws will be decided in the course of a few years by sovereign people of the United States of America in their paramount power and sovereignty, to be null and void, mere debris that you have thrown over the Constitution. They will be swept away from it."* **Thomas Hendricks a Democrat** from Indiana added, *" I do not believe that the Negro race and the white race can mingle in the exercise of political power and bring good results to society. We are of* *different races. Men may argue about it as much as they please; we know that in many respects there is a great difference between the races. There is a difference not only in their physical appearance and conformation, but there is a difference morally and intellectually, and I do not believe that the two races can mingle successfully in the management of government. I do not believe that they will add to the common intelligence of the country when we make them voters."* **Republican Senator William Stewart** said, *"This Amendment is a declaration to make all men, without regard to race or color, equal before the law. The arguments in favor of it are so numerous and so convincing that they carry conviction to every mind. It is the only measure that will really abolish slavery...."* **Republican Senator James Patterson of New Hampshire said:** *"I hope that this proposition will be adopted, for all the amendments which have been offered I think it is the best. Our object is to meet a wrong done to a class of black native citizens; to give them the same privileges that other citizens of the United States possess...."* Debates took place on January 11, 1869.

The Enforcement Act of 1870

The Purpose: The new Bill was introduced by **Republican Congressman John Bingham of Ohio**. He said the purpose of the bill was to enforce the legal right of the citizen of the United States to vote in the several States of this Union – a right which had been defiantly denied in violation of the Constitution.

Democrat's Opposition: The Democrats opposed the legislation, because it was designed to force compliance with the Fifteenth Amendment. **James Bayard, the Democrat of Delaware said**, *"...This bill is intended not to prevent discrimination between various races of men, but to discriminate directly **against the white race in favor of the black race**.... I consider this bill not an act of "appropriate legislation fairly to enforce that amendment, but it is* *only another attempt to bolster up by violence, intimidation, in the shape of penal enactments, the inferior capacities of the Negro race in the struggle for racial and political equality.... Now, sir, for whom has all this been done? For whose protection? It has been only for the ignorant, semi-barbarous race unfit for voting, manufactured into votes and allies of the Republican Party to sustain themselves a little longer in power...."*

Senator William Stewart of Nevada responded: *"Mr. President, I congratulate the Senate and the country that we are about to assert some of the powers of Congress for the protection of voters; for the protection of down-trodden; for the protection of persons in their political and civil rights; that we are about to get a bill which asserts something of dignity and power of this action.*

It has been stated by some, in the course of the debate, that no legislation is necessary, and by others that this Fifteenth Amendment is a fraud and shall be of short duration. I tell the Opposition that it is no fraud, and that its duration will be perpetual. Rights guaranteed and granted to the people cannot be taken from them. No party can stand on the basis of taking away such rights. When the high sounding phase came from certain pretended or real leaders of the Democratic Party that they intended to acquiesce in the Fifteenth Amendment, I did not then believe in the good faith of the declaration so made. The states which have come from the other side since this debate has begun, convinced me that I was right; that they did not intend to do it in good faith....

...We have commenced legislation in the right direction by attempting to guard the ballot-box in New York against the trampling of it down by the Democratic Party. Why should the gentlemen talk about our want of faith in the people? Sir, our faith in the people is unlimited; but we have no faith in a Democratic oligarchy in New York City or New Orleans or Georgia, which by its power shall drive loyal men from the polls....

Ever since the war closed you have been trying to point out how we could not reconstruct. You have been quibbling and complaining at every attempt we have made. You have been occupying whole nights here in uttering condemnations of the just and the liberal measures of a patriotic Congress. You have failed and you will fail again. Let me advise you now to turn your attention to enforcing the laws, to turn your attention to the only means by which peace can be had, and we will meet you in brotherly love. We have no enmity against the Democratic Party as such, but while it goes wrong, while its motto is anarchy, injustice, inequality, fraud, we will conquer it every time.... Your now fighting the Fifteenth Amendment is only another of your usual blunders.... Come out on the side of humanity, justice, peace, law, the Constitution; take the Constitution as it is, uphold it, and defend it, and you will have peace...." Debates took place on May 16, 1870.

The Force Act of 1871

The Purpose: The propose of the Force Act of 1871 was to supplement the 1870 Enforcement Act by supplying an independent enforcement machinery which would affirmatively insure vindication of the right to vote in all congressional elections. The machinery contemplated was to be provided by the appointment of federal officials to supervise the election process in each election district (in cities and towns with over 20, 000 inhabitants)

Democrat's Opposition: **Charles Eldredge a Democrat** from Wisconsin opened up the debate with these words: *"Of all the legislation proposed by this or any other Congress, there is none, in my judgement, more unwarrantable and unjustifiable than that proposed by this bill. It is absolutely atrocious. It is hideous and revolting.... It provides a system to drive citizens from the polls, and to disgust all honest men with our elections.... By conferring suffrage upon the colored race have we lost the rights our fathers secured to us by the Constitution? **In giving freedom to the slaves have we become slaves ourselves?"*** The Democrats dominated the debates, only a few Republicans were able to speak. **John**

Churchill a Republican from New York was one of the few who spoke. He said, *"For some years past grave doubts have prevailed in different portion of this country as to whether the declared results of the elections truly expressed the will of the people.... The object of this bill is simply to perfect the bill of last summer and to make it more likely to accomplish the real objective of which was desired and intended to be accomplished by it. And that is, that while it shall exclude no honest man from the polls and hinder no honest man in his effort to vote, it shall prevent the repetition of such acts and many other acts of offense against the elective ranchise as have been detailed...."* **(Debates took place on February 15, 1871)**

Ku Klux Klan Act of 1871

The Purpose: To stop the Klan's *terrorist activities* against Blacks and their White supporters (Republicans), primarily in the south. The law was designed to (1) provide civil and criminal sanctions to deter infringements upon civil rights; and (2) to provide authority to the government to meet with force unlawful combinations and violence which interfered with civil rights or the execution of justice or federal law.

Democrat's Opposition: George Morgan a Democratic Congressman from Ohio said, *"I maintain that if such offenses are committed they have been caused in good part by the mistaken legislation of Congress.... Now sir, if you want to preserve peace to the South, if you want to preserve peace and tranquillity to the whole country, if you are not determined to strike a blow which may end the total subversion of our free institutions, change your policy to the South."*

Senator William Stoughton, the Republican from Michigan countered with the following words: *"The evidence taken before the Senate committee in relations to the outrages, lawlessness and violence in North Carolina establishes the following propositions:*

1. *The Ku Klux Klan organization* [which] *exists throughout the State, has a political purpose, and is composed of the members of the* **Democratic or Conservative Party.**

2. This organization has sought to carry out its purposes by murders, whippings, intimidation, and violence against it opponents.

3. It not only binds its members to execute decrees of crime, but protects them against conviction and punishment, first by disguises and secrecy, and second, by perjury, if necessary, upon the witness-stand and in the jury box.

4. All of the offenders in this order, which has established reign of **terrorism** and bloodshed throughout the State not one has yet been convicted."

During an interview with a Klan member by the name of James E. Boyd, he told the Senate Investigation Committee that he was *"initiated into the Ku Klux Klan* **as an auxiliary of the Democratic Party"**

Stoughton continues: *"We may concede, Mr. Speaker, that if this system of violence is to continue in the South, the Democratic Party will secure the ascendancy. If political opponents can be marked for slaughter by secret bands of cowardly assassins who ride forth with impunity to execute the decrees upon the unarmed and defenseless, it will be fatal alike to the Republican Party and civil liberty. But sir, we may well ask where will this end? How long will it be before the Tammany Hall Democracy, who are now furnishing arms to the Ku Klux Klan of the South to murder southern Republicans, will introduce this new element of Democratic success into the northern politics?*

During an interview with a Negro who was a victim of the Klan, he told the Senate Investigation Committee how he was shot and left for dead:

"*...The one* [Klan] *said, "open the door."*

"I said, I shouldn't do it."

Then one said, "blow his brains out."

"Just as he said that they all fired through the door.... They shot a half a dozen times or more. I clapped my hand on here

[placing his hand on his breast] *and said, "they've shot me. My boy knew where there were some loose planks in the floor. He jerked up two of them and they all run through under the house— all the biggest of them, but the three little girls I had.*

Question: *"What occurred afterwards?"*

Answer: *"The next morning I sent for the doctor to come and take out the balls* [gun shots]. *Dr. Montgomery came and took out the balls and told them they had better move me to Graham... or else they won't move me at all. That evening they carried me to Graham and got me there at night."*

Question: *"How many balls did they fire into you?"*

Answer: *"There were five balls."* [The witness indicated where he had been shot – in both arms and in his chest.]

Question: *"What has been the effect of such proceedings upon the colored people of that county. Do they feel safe?"*

Answer: *"They don't feel safe there at all. I can tell you that a great many of them have taken the notion to leave.... They wanted to run them all off because the principal part of them voted the Radical* [Republican] *ticket."*

Question: *"Wanted to run all of them off who voted the Radical Ticket?"*

Answer: *"Yes, sir."*

Question: *"Did you hear that said?"*

Answer: *"Yes, sir, I heard it talked and I saw them try it. They tried to turn me from voting the Republican ticket, but I didn't turn and that is why they shot me.... That is the case every election that has been there. They have been trying to get us to vote the Conservative* [Democratic] *ticket...."*

Question: *"Were those that would not vote the Conservative ticket the ones that had these outrages committed against them?"*

Answer: *"Yes, sir. You never saw one bothered at all that voted the Conservative Ticket."*

After sharing these interviews with the Senate, **Senator Stoughton** went on to say; *"The report, Mr. Speaker to which I have referred shows over one hundred and fifty authenticated cases where person have either been murdered, brutally beaten, or driven away at the peril of their lives. The Democratic Party first denied their association, then excused the outrages. In Tennessee and other southern states, the laws passed by Republican Legislatures to suppress and punish the Ku Klux Klan were repealed as soon as the Democratic Party came back into power. The relation of the Democratic Party to the Klan is precisely that of the receiver of stolen property to the thief. The murder of leading Republicans, terrifying the colored population and putting whole neighborhoods in fear so that the Klan can control an election is heralded as a Democratic victory. How long will it be before this party who are now furnishing arms to the Klan of the South to murder Southern Republicans, will introduce this new element of Democratic success into northern politics? A few days ago, over 100 Alabama Klansmen made a raid on upon Meridian Mississippi, and carried off their victims for execution."* **The Republican Congressman from Mississippi (George McKee)** responded, *"Mr. Speaker, I did not intend to take part in this debate but statements have been made upon this floor that demand refutation. The Meridian massacre was in my own district. It has often been alluded to in this debate, and I cannot pass it in silence. The Alabama Klan has made frequent incursions into our State. They participated in this bloody massacre at Meridian, invited there by our home Ku Klux. They had been in that County before that time. Prior to the late butchery, two colored officials had been murdered. Other outrages had been committed, but still it was deemed that enough had not been* *done, and the bloody work of death culminated in that infamous scene of riot and blood at Meridian which can neither be denied or excused."*

"I do not care to go into details. One single statement tells the whole story. One, and perhaps two white men killed, eight or ten colored men killed according to the Democratic authority, while Republicans claim that twenty five or thirty have been killed in the streets and shot or hung in the swamps; and yet amongst all this red list of slaughter you do not find the name of a single Democrat. The dead and wounded, the maimed and the scourged, are all, all Republicans." Debates took place on March 28, 1871.

1875 Jim Crow Laws

Southern Democrats of Tennessee legislated our nation's first Jim Crow Laws. The law mandated that blacks be confined to separate sections of trains, depots and wharves. Southern states under Democratic control expanded the use of such laws to include many other facilities as well, including separate restrooms, drinking fountains, public parks and cemeteries. Eventually blacks were banned from white barbershops, hotels, restaurants, theaters and in some states they were required to swear on separate Bibles in courtroom proceedings. The Jim Crow Laws along with the new Black Codes (both initiated by Southern Democrats) had a devastating impact on the newly freed slaves. Some historian believed that these laws and codes created conditions far worse than slavery.

1875 Civil Rights Act

The Purpose: *"To obtain equality in Public Accommodations. The law stated the following: Be it enacted by the Senate and House of Representatives of the United States of America in Congress assembled. That all persons within the jurisdiction of the United*

States shall be entitled to the full and equal enjoyment of the accommodation, advantages, facilities and privileges of inns, public conveyances on land or water, theaters, and other places amusement; subject only to the conditions and limitation established by law, and applicable alike to citizens of every race and color, regardless of any previous condition of servitude...."

Democrat's Opposition: The bill was introduced by **Republican Senator Charles Sumner**. He died in March 1874 one year before the bill was passed. **Republican Senator Frederick Frelinghuysen of New Jersey** opened up the debate. The Senator said, "*There is but one idea in the bill, and that is: The equality of races before the law. The language of this bill secures full and equal privileges in schools subject to laws which do not discriminate as to color. The bill provides that full and equal privileges shall be enjoyed by all persons in public schools supported by taxation, subject only to the limitation established by law, applicable alike to citizens of every race and color and regardless of previous servitude. The object of the bill is to destroy, not recognize the distinctions of race.*" **Willard Saulsbury a Democrat from Delaware** responded. " *...There is coming a day when the American people will hold you and your party* [Republican] *to a strict responsibility for present indifference to their wishes and for the great wrong you propose by this bill to inflict upon them.*

What is this measure? Disguise it as you may, it is nothing more nor less than an attempt on the part of the American Congress to enforce association and companionship between the races in this country. The object of this bill is not to confer upon the color race any political rights. It proposes to enforce familiarity, association, and companionship between the white and colored people of this country. Is not that true?

That is the object of this bill. It proposes so far as hotels are concerned that the white and the colored people shall have the save advantages, equal advantages; that they shall enter with equal right into every part of the inn; that the keeper of the inn shall make no discrimination on account of their race or color; that *colored men shall sit at the same table beside the white guest, that he shall enter the same parlor and take his seat beside the **wife and daughter of the white man**, whether the white man is willing or not, because you prohibit discrimination against him.*

If the object was not to enforce companionship, why do you not permit in this bill the landlord to set apart a portion of the parlor for white people, so that he might have one table for the colored man and another table for the white man, giving to one as good accommodations as the other? Why is it that there is not a provision which allows that? Simply because, I say, the object and purpose of this bill is force association and companionship between the races." The debates took place April 29 – May 22, 1874.

The Repeal Act of 1894

The Purpose: After the Democrats won the Presidency and both houses in 1892, they attempted to repeal important civil rights legislation. They introduced this bill to repeal all statues relating to supervisors of elections and deputy marshals, as well as federal protection of the right to vote.

Republican Opposition: Leading the debate against the bill included: Republican Congressman Marriott Brosius of Pennsylvania and Republican Senator George Hoar, of Massachusetts. On October 10, 1893 it passed in the House with 201 voting for it and 102 against it. On February 7, 1894 it passed in the Senate. Thirty-nine voted for it and 28 voted against it.

Just before the final vote, **Senator Hoar of Massachusetts** presented the following argument:

"Wherever there is a crevice in our protection of the freedom of the ballot there you will find the Democratic Party trying to break through. Where ever we have left open an opportunity to get possession of an office contrary to the true and constitutional will of the majority there you will find that party pressing; there you will find that party exercising an ingenuity before which even the

*great inventive genius of American People exerted in other direc-
tions fails and is insignificant in the comparison.*

*In one State, Mississippi, in order to disfranchise Republicans
who can not read and write and let Democrats who can not read and
write vote, there is a constitutional provision by which Democratic
election officers determine whether the understanding of the voters
who can not read or write is a fit and sufficient understanding of the
Constitution; and, although that was denounced by able Democrats
holding high public positions both in Washington and Mississippi,
the proposition finds defenders on this floor, Senators gravely com-
paring it to the provision of the constitution of Massachusetts....*

*In Delaware, it is necessary that a tax should be paid a cer-
tain time before hand, and, accordingly, unless they are much
belied, the Democratic tax collector runs away when the Republican come to pay their taxes....*

*"Mr. President, this is a question of fraud or no fraud. They
tell us that there have been some Republican invasions of the elective franchise, and it is quite possible, but where can you find one
well-authenticated case of a man who has been deprived or incon-
venienced in the exercise of his franchise by these United States
marshals or other officers, I will pledge myself to find ten thousand well established by evidence on record here where without
those securities Republicans have been deprived of their votes by
Democratic practices. I incur no danger in making that challenge. If you will produce me a citizen of the United States, a Democrat, who lost his honest vote in consequence of intimidation or
impediment, created by these United States marshals, I will find on
record here the proof of ten thousand Republicans who have lost
their votes by Democratic practices....*

*Mr. President, the nation must protect its own. Every citizen
whose right is imperiled if he be but one, when it is a right of
national citizenship and a right conferred and enjoyed under the
Constitution of the United States, has the right to demand for its
protection the entire force of the United States until the Army has
spent its last man and the Navy fired its last gun. Most of us have*

nothing else than the right to vote.... The urn in which the American cast his ballot ought to be, aye, and it shall be, as sacred as a sacramental vessel."

1875-1956: The Silent Legislative Years

From 1875 to 1956, there were various civil rights bills introduced into Congress but none were ever passed. The seventy-five years of legislative apathy was marked with 75 years of lynchings, beatings, and harsh imprisonment, all initiated by those who supported the so-called *"plank"* of the *"re-organized Democratic Party."* **Senator Ben Tillman of South Carolina** told America: *"We reorganized the Democratic Party with one plank, and the only plank, namely, that this is a white man's country, and white men must govern it."* The following are just a few of the incidents that took place during these years.

In **1898**, The Democrats carried out their political objectives in Wilmington North Carolina, when they successfully drove Black Republicans out of office by rigging the 1898 election, and killing several blacks. The Democrat's campaign theme was: "saving our white women" [from the middle class Blacks who controlled Wilmington at the time]. Shortly after the Wilmington riots, riots broke out in other parts of the south, 101 blacks were lynched.

By the turn of the century, thousands of blacks (in the South) were placed in hardcore prison labor camps. According to historians, the prison camps were worse than slavery - and represented a new resource of free forced labor. The prisoners were required to work from 10 to 14 hours a day, six to seven days a week in temperatures above 100 degrees and below zero. One-fourth of the prison population, were black children ages 6 to 18. Twelve-year old Cy Williams, was sentenced to 20 years of hard labor for allegedly stealing a horse that he was too small to ride. Eight-year old Will Evens was sentenced to 2 years of hard labor for taking some change from a counter, and six-year old Mary Gay was sentenced to 30 days of hard labor for taking a hat. While southern authorities sent whites to *jail* for the same offenses (with shorter sentences), they sent blacks to the prison labor camps with longer sentences. The camps provided free labor for building railroads, for draining snake and alligator infested swamps and rivers, and for mining coal. Conditions in these camps were harsh - blacks were transported from one project to another in rolling cages, similar to those used for circus animals. While thousands died from malaria, frost bites, heat strokes, and shackle poisoning, others were buried alive in mines, blown to pieces during mine explosions, and many others were drowned or shot and beaten to death. Every southern black was a potential prisoner, which meant that the southern owners of railroads and mines had an unlimited resource of free labor. Historians say the prison system was merely a new form slavery—but more inhumane than the previous period of slavery.

In **1900**, one hundred blacks were lynched in the democratically controlled South.

1900-1917 there were several terrorist attacks on blacks, in Alabama, Georgia, Louisiana and other parts of the south. Several thousand blacks were lynched, beaten, and shot to death during this period.

In **1904**, Thomas Dixon opened his new stage play (The Klansman) in Atlanta Georgia. The play glorified the Klan and portrayed blacks as savaged men on the prowl for white women. During the week of September 17th, an Atlanta newspaper falsely reported rapes of a few white women. Their false reports resulted in several thousand white men gathering in the streets of Atlanta, mercifully beating blacks at random. When blacks fought back, they were killed. The Militia was called in to control the riot.

In **1909,** three whites that opposed the Democrat's racist practices, and the lynching of blacks, started the NAACP. According to Juan Williams, author of <u>Thurgood Marshall: American Revolutionary</u>, as the NAACP grew, it depended heavily on white Republican philanthropist for its financial support.

In **1912**, W.E.B Dubois endorsed Democratic candidate, Woodrow Wilson for President. He asked Wilson to support black education, blacks' rights to vote and own land, and to stop the onslaught of lynchings. Shortly after Wilson took office, the Democratic President gave his blessings to three southern cabinet members to segregate their departments. A New York paper released an article entitled: "Jim Crow had come to Washington." One government supervisor boasted that, "There are no government positions for Negroes in the South, a Negroes place is in the cornfield."

In **1915,** the stage play, "The Klansman" was made into a motion picture, entitled; "The Birth of a Nation." The movie strengthened the Klan and its membership grew. In many places where the Democrats ruled, gangs of Whites openly attacked blacks on the street, after watching the movie.

In **1917**, black soldiers in Houston, Texas who had been harassed for several months by the Houston police, took matters into their own hands after one of their soldiers was arrested and beaten without cause. One hundred black soldiers went to town to retaliate. Shots were fired. Sixteen whites and four fellow soldiers were killed. Nineteen soldiers were court-martialed and sentenced to death. The soldiers were denied the right to appeal their case to Woodrow Wilson, the Democratic President whom *W.E.B Dubois had previously endorsed.*

May 1918, there were a series of lynching in Georgia. When Mary Turner, who was nine-months pregnant complained that she was going to see to it that the white men who lynched her husband would be prosecuted, the mob drug her from her home, tortured and hung her. While she was still alive, hanging from the rope, they cut open her womb so child would spill out, then set her on fire and waited for the two to die.

1919 - During the Senate debates on the Ku Klux Klan Act of 1871, Republican Senator, William Stoughton asked the following question. "How long will it before the Tammany Hall Democracy, who are now furnishing arms to the Ku Klux Klan of the south to murder southern Republicans, will introduce this new element of

Democratic success into the **northern politics?**" His question was answered on July 27, 1919, when whites attacked and killed, Eugene Williams a black swimmer in Chicago. When the dust settled, 15 whites and 23 blacks were killed. "Jim Crow," says the Chicago Tribune, "has come north."

In **1919**, in Elaine Arkansas, there were reports that as many as 200 black farmers were massacred, while several others were arrested and executed, simply because they met at a black church to discuss how they could stop their white landlords from cheating them out of their cotton crops.

On **May 31, 1921**, Tulsa's leading newspaper (Tulsa Tribune) released a front-page article alleging that a black man had raped a white woman. Whites went on a rampage, killing 300 blacks, wounding 800 others, arresting as many as 6,000. During the riot, whites burned down 35 city blocks in the middle class black community (which was also known as the Greenwood District or Black Wall Street).

On December 31, 1922, a young white woman from Rosewood, Florida claimed she was raped by a black man. The next day (New Years 1923) several whites from nearby communities swarmed the town killing over 100 blacks and burning down most of the black owned businesses and homes. The massacre included women and children. Others escaped by spending the night in the swamps. Democratic Governor Cary Hardee, took no action.

In **1933**, Democratic candidate, Franklin D. Roosevelt received the black vote and became President of the United States. Professor John Hope Franklin says, shortly after taking office, blacks "discovered that agencies of the federal government were as capable of discriminatory practices or could be used for such purposes, as any others. Black sharecroppers and tenants had difficulty in obtaining relief benefits from the Agricultural Administration because landlords kept their relief checks. While the Federal Housing Authority guaranteed a limited number of loans for Negroes to build or purchase homes, its policy was not to interfere with local housing practices that excluded Negroes from

certain neighborhoods. Lynchings and other forms of racial violence had continued during the New Deal and the federal government had pleaded that it had no jurisdiction over such matters."
*President Roosevelt also banned black newspapers from the mili-
tary claiming they were* "communist." *These were the same newspapers that urged their readers to vote Democrat.*

In **1945**, Harry S. Truman, a Democrat, was elected President
of the United States. President Truman started the process of inte-
grating the military, but no Civil Rights legislation was passed during his administration to stop the continued lynchings and terrorist
attacks by the southern Democrats and their Klan supporters. Historians report that southern blacks lived in constant fear, knowing that
death at the hands of the terrorist was just a matter of time.

May 17, 1954 the Democrats received a major defeat when
the United States Supreme Court rendered its decision on Brown v
Board of Education.   Southern Democrats were furious, but continued to practice segregation.

Black historians told the producers of the PBS's series: "The
Rise & Fall of Jim Crow" that in a Democratically controlled south,
blacks accepted the fact that one day they would all die from terrorist attacks, *"they just didn't know how or when."* Throughout
this 75-year period, Blacks lived in constant terror, day and night.
Their future seemed hopeless. Then in 1954, a ray of hope came
with *Brown v the Board of Education* and three years later, more
encouragement came with the introduction of the Civil Rights Act
of 1957. Too many, this was the dawning of a new day.

1957 Civil Rights

Purpose: Introduced by Republican President, Dwight D.
Eisenhower and supported by a bipartisan Congress, the law was
designed to establish a Civil Rights Commission and permit the
government to bring lawsuits for civil rights violations, including
the denial of the right to vote.

Democrat's Opposition: Southern Democrats voiced the strongest opposition to this bill. **William Winstead, the Democrat from Mississippi** opening remarks included the following: *"This bill contains most of the evil provisions of last years so-called civil rights bill, plus an additional section which would empower the Attorney General of the United States, to seek injunctions in the Federal district court for the enforcement of alleged violations of civil rights laws."*

Richard Russell the Democratic Senator from Georgia argued: *" This law will be administered by a politically minded Attorney General. There can be little doubt that he will be constantly pressed by the Vice President of the United States to apply the great powers of the law in the Southern States, at such places and in such time and manner* **as the NAACP, of which the Vice President is the most distinguished member, may demand**.

The threat of this vicious legislation will be used to intimate honest officials of the State and local governments who are earnestly endeavoring to discharge their duties under their oaths of the office and the laws of their respective States.

It is entirely likely that the application of **this law will result in forcing the registration of a large number of Negro citizens who, in fact, cannot meet the qualifications prescribed for all electors under the laws of the State in which they live.** *It is a thoroughly bad bill, and places dangerous powers in the hands of those who are to administer it without much comforting proof of their responsibility and fairness."*

In the Senate opponents were successful in eliminating Part III of the bill which was aimed at striking down the separation of the races in hospitals, schools, in hotels, at swimming pools and places of public entertainment. Senator Russell went on to say. *"As I have said, the bill is bad, but consider how much worse it would have been if we had not been able to eliminate Part III.*

If the original Part III had been applied so as to **bring about the social intermingling of the races from the kindergarten to the grave***, southern civilization would have destroyed beyond hope of* *redemption. This was the supreme tragedy we sought above all else to avert."*

William Colmer, the Democratic Congressman from Mississippi said, *"Some of us have conscientiously and therefore stubbornly opposed this misnamed civil-rights proposal. It is nothing more or less than the abolition of the Civil Rights of all the people under the guise of granting civil rights to a highly organized and politically powerful minority group. So, Mr. Speaker, as we gather today in this historic Chamber to witness the final act in the tragedy of the beginning of the downfall of the Republic, it might be well to briefly sum up the value of the winners and losers in this political gamble.*

The actors in this political tragedy are of the summit stature in both political camps, **It is obvious that the Republican high command has deliberately set out to recapture the minority Negro vote <u>stolen</u> from them by the Democratic high command some two decades ago."*

Clifford Case, Republican from New Jersey: *"Mr. President, the facts which have been developed in debate in the House and in the Senate, indicated clearly the deprivation of voting rights that exist in this country and the need for further legislation for the enforcement of those rights.... It is particularly appropriate, Mr. President, that these further remedies be by the way of preventive relief. As I indicated earlier, it does not do a person who has been deprived of his right to vote any good to have the person who deprives him of the right, put in jail, and no amount of money damages can compensate a person deprived of the right to vote for that deprivation. In spite of the existence of these theoretical remedies, the right to vote has been taken away from millions of our citizens. It is clear that an additional remedy is require."* Debates took place June 5-18, 1957 in the House and from August 29-30 in the Senate.

1960 Civil Rights Act

The Purpose: On February 5. 1960, President Dwight D. Eisenhower sent to Congress a message requesting, *"legislation to strengthen the law dealing with obstruction of justice so as to provide expressly that the use of force or threats of force to obstruct court orders in school desegregation cases shall be a federal offense."* He said, *"there have been instances where extremist have attempted to by mob violence and other concerted threats of violence to obstruct the accomplishment of objectives in school decrees."*

Democrat's Opposition: Like the 1957 Civil Rights Act, this bill had bi-partisan support. In his argument for the bill, **Democratic Congressman Ray Madden of Indiana said**, *"Patriotic Negroes of America only ask that their future generations are not called upon to combat the economic and educational impediments which their ancestors endured."*

Congressman **Overton Brooks, a Democrat from Louisiana countered and said**, *"This Civil Rights bill is as vicious an instrument as I have read since I have been in this Congress. If enacted into law, it will undoubtedly hurt our people in the South. The bill provides that anybody who writes a letter critical of a decree of the Federal courts dealing with the integration of schools, with the intent to obstruct the execution of an order of this court, is guilty of a Federal crime and punishable by fine and imprisonment. **The provision regarding fleeing from one State to another to avoid prosecution or imprisonment for the crime of bombing or setting fire to a building, whether it be church or otherwise, make another step toward <u>taking away from States their fundamental rights.</u>** "* **Congressman William McCulloch a Republican from Ohio** argued, *"For almost a century, the failure to provide political equality for all qualified citizens has been nagging the conscience of the people, and now we are obliged to consider and pass legislation to insure and implement such rights to all qualified citizens, which rights so long ago, were extended to all, only* *to be lost or taken away, in a substantial number of states or lesser political subdivision of our country."*

1964 Civil Rights Act

The purpose: One of the prime authors and sponsors of the final version of this bill was Senator Everett Dirksen of Illinois. The law which contained 11 different Titles, prohibited discrimination in all public accommodations, if their operation *"affected commerce (including hotels and other places of lodging of more than five rooms, restaurants and other eating places, gasoline stations, theaters, motion pictures houses, stadiums and other places of exhibitions or entertainment)."* It also covered voting, desegregation of public education, Equal Opportunity and a Civil Rights Commission.

Background Leading Up to 1964 Civil Rights Acts

In his book, *Why We Can't Wait*, Dr. Martin Luther King said, **the feeling was growing among Negroes that the [Kennedy] administration had oversimplified and underestimated the civil rights issue**.... *The administration had fashioned its primary approach to discrimination in the South....* **With each new Negro protest <u>we were advised</u>, sometimes privately and sometimes in public, <u>to call off our efforts</u>** *and channel all of our energies into registering voters. On each occasion we would agree with the importance of voting rights, but would patiently seek to explain that Negroes did not want to neglect all other rights while one was selected for concentrated attention.* **Kennedy administration appeared to believe it had by it positive deeds, earned enough credit to coast on civil rights**.... *"* King went on to say, *"that no one would have ever believed that during the first two years of the Kennedy administration"* (1961-1962) that Negroes *"would become as militant as the segregationist."* What King referring to was the social unrest that African Americans vehemently expressed during the first two years of the Kennedy administration.

- **In 1961**, Freedom Riders were attacked and arrested in the south. The Freedom Riders were organized by CORE to test desegregation orders in the south. Black protested and Robert Kennedy ordered 600 Federal Marshals to Montgomery, Alabama to maintain order.

- **In 1962**, several thousand federal troops were ordered to the University of Mississippi to maintain order as riots erupted as whites protested the admission of James Meredith, a 29-year old black veteran.

- **In 1962**, Black churches in Georgia were burned to discourage voter registration.

- **In 1963**, the nation was in chaos, the situation was out of control. By the week of May 18th the Department of Justice had noted that there had been *forty-three* different civil rights demonstrations of various magnitudes. On April 3[rd,] Dr. King demonstrated in Birmingham, Alabama. The numbers of demonstrators increased significantly by May 3rd. There were more demonstrations after Medgar Evers, a civil rights leader was assassinated in Mississippi. By May 7th - over 2500 demonstrators had been arrested, many of them were children. May 11th a black leader's home was bombed. During that same period, Democratic Governor, George Wallace refused to comply with a presidential order to register two black students to the University of Alabama.

New York University Law School Professor, Bernard Schwartz said, *"The events in Birmingham, followed by the need to federalize the Alabama National Guard to frustrate George*

*Wallace, the Democratic Governor of Alabama, whose efforts to thwart a court order admitting two Negro students to the state university roused the national conscience, as almost never before, to the need for speedy action to correct the situation. Most important perhaps, they stimulated **a previously lukewarm Administration** to becoming firm supporters of strong civil rights legislation. **The tepid attitude of President John Kennedy in the matter had been a source of serious discomfort to many of his supporters.** ...The troubles in Alabama completely altered the Administration's attitude to make a full commitment to Civil rights that, **he had until then, so carefully avoided.*** On June 19, 1963 President Kennedy sent the following letter to Congress. The first section of the letter seem to suggest that the President was more concerned with the social disorder that was taking place, than he was about the deplorable conditions of the African Americans.

President's Kennedy Message to Congress
For Passage of 1963 Civil Rights Act
June 19, 1963

*"Last week I addressed to the American people an appeal to conscience—a request for their cooperation in meeting the growing moral crisis in American race relations. I warned of 'a **rising tide of discontent that threatens the public safety**" in many parts of the country. I emphasized that "the events in Birmingham and elsewhere have so increased the cries for equality that **no city or state or legislative body can prudently choose to <u>ignore</u> them."*** *"It is a time to act," I said, "in the Congress, in State and local legislative bodies and, above all, in all of our daily lives."*

*In the days that have followed, **the predictions of increased violence have been tragically borne out.** The "fires of frustration and discord" have burned hotter than ever.*

At the same time, the response of the American people to this appeal to their principles and obligations has been reassuring. Private progress—by merchants and the unions and local organizations—has been marked, if not uniform in many areas. Many doors long closed to Negroes, North and South, have been open. Local biracial committees, under private and public sponsorship, have mushroomed. The mayors of our major cities, whom I earlier addressed, have pledged renewed action. **But persisting inequalities and tensions make it clear that Federal action must lead the way,** *providing both the Nation's standard and a nationwide solution. In short, the time has come for Congress of the United States to join with the executive and judicial branches in making it clear to all that race has no place in American life or law....*

The result of continued Federal legislative inaction will be continued, if not increased, racial strife—causing the leadership on both sides to pass from the hands of reasonable responsible men to **the purveyors of hate and violence, endangering domestic tranquility,** *retarding our Nation's economic and social progress and weakening the respect with which the rest of the world regards us. No American, I feel sure, would prefer this course of* **tension, disorder, and division**—*and the great majority of our citizens simply cannot accept it.*

For these reasons, *I am proposing that Congress stay in session this year until it has enacted—preferable as a single omnibus bill—the most responsible, reasonable, and urgently needed solutions to this problem, solutions which should be acceptable to all fair-minded men. This bill would be known as the Civil Rights Act of 1963...."*

President Kennedy died before the bill was passed. His successor, President Lyndon Johnson, had a difficult time convincing his own party that such legislation was necessary. Because of the strong opposition by the Southern Democrats, the debates involving this bill lasted over eighty days. The debates took up some 7,000 pages in the Congressional Record (consisting of over 10,000,000 words) and created the longest filibuster in Senate history. The following are a few who opposed it and those who supported it.

Democrat's Opposition: This was another bill that received bi-partisan support. Democrats who opposed the bill included **Donald Matthews from Florida**. In his arguments he said, *"In the name of Civil Rights, this bill would deprive schoolchildren of milk and basic education if there appears to be discrimination because of race, color, or national origin. How cruel can the humanitarians and the moralist be in the name of Civil Rights? What do we mean by discrimination? The communist have been fed under Republican and Democratic administrations, but this will deny daily bred to American Children in the name of Civil Rights."*

Thomas Abernethy a Democrat from Mississippi, argued, *"If enacted, it is certain to precipitate a tremendous upheaval in our society, but not the kind of upheaval that proponents apparently expect. I predict it will precipitate an upheaval that will make the sit-ins, kneel-ins, lie-ins, mass picketing, chanting, the march on Washington, and all other elements of the **so-called Negro revolutions**, all of these—I predict—will look like kindergarten play in comparison with the counter-revolutions that is bound to arise and continue to grow and grow, and grow."*

Howard Smith, a Democrat from Virginia added the following arguments: *"I deeply regret that out of the 15 minutes allotted to me, I cannot assign time for protest to the many patriotic Members of this House who would like to express their distaste, dismay and disgust at this invasion of the rights of American citizens. In a few minutes, you will vote this monstrous instrument of oppression upon all of the American People.... Be forewarned that **the paid agents and leaders of the NAACP can never permit this law to be gradually and peacefully accepted because that means an end to their well-paid activities.**"*

Democrat Robert Byrd from [West Virginia] said, *"Can the Senator from Minnesota [Humphrey] assure the Senator from West Virginia that under title VI school children may not be bused from one end of the community to another end of the community at the taxpayers' expense to relieve **so-called** racial imbalance in the schools?*

Democrat Sam Ervin said, *"This bill is based upon a strange thesis. The thesis is that the best way and the only way to promote the civil rights of some Americans is to rob all Americans of Civil Rights equally precious, and to reduce the supposedly Sovereign States to meaningless zeros on the Nation's map."*

Olin Johnston the Democrat from South Carolina argued, *"Mr. President, this is indeed the blackest day in the U.S. Senate since 1875, when the Congress passed a civil rights bill similar to this one. It was 89 years ago that the* [Republican] *Congress passed the nefarious Reconstruction era civil rights laws,* **identical with what we are now discussing,** *which were later declared unconstitutional by the U.S. Supreme Court. The Senate, if it passes this measure before us, will be compounding that unconstitutional error made back in* 1875 [when the Republicans passed the 1875 Civil Rights Act]. *I predict that this bill will never be enforced without turning our Nation into a police state and without the cost of bloodshed and violence.*

Ten years ago, in 1954, the Supreme Court took it upon itself to amend The Constitution of the United States and declared that segregation – that is, required separate but equal school facilities for the races – was illegal. Instead of promoting peace and harmony between the races, as a result of this decision we have seen racial violence, intolerance, bigotry, and hatred compounded and multiplied. Whenever Government decrees a social policy for people when people are not behind such a policy, one can only expect as a result such violence and trouble."

Those who advocate passage of this Civil Rights bill need not expect this legislation to do anything for our country except to divide our people and rekindle the hatreds and prejudices of 100 years ago, to be perpetuated into the future for at least another 100 years. Contained in this legislation is not just a so so-called framework for engendering equality among people of different races. This bill contains the equipment, tools, temptation and power to establish a vast Federal network for controlling the people of every community. The damage this will do to our Government is incomprehensible....

When one talks of eliminating discrimination with this piece of so-called legislation, if it were not such a serious matter it would be fit for a good joke....

*If we sweep away the clutter of emotion and the clatter of the demonstrators and look at the legal aspect of this legislation, we can only come to the realistic conclusion that **it is unconstitutional and will be recorded in history as the greatest robber of the rights of individuals and States and the most tremendous hoax ever perpetrated upon the people of the United States. "***

John Sparkman the Democrat from Alabama told Congress: *"Mr. President, we now have before us a motion to proceed with the consideration of H.R. 7152, **the so called civil rights bill**....*

Mr. President, never in my long history of opposition to so-called civil rights legislation have I risen to attack so formidable an array of legislation that is probably well-intended but which could do so much to take away many of the liberties and rights for which we have fought throughout the history of this Nation....

...For months I have been receiving literally thousands of letter from all over the Nation supporting my stand against this bill. So I rise not just with a mandate from the people of Alabama, or the South. My mandate comes from the four corners of the country....

Title II, the so-called public accommodations provision of H.R. 7152 is the most sweeping, the most far-reaching attempt to repeal the constitutional concept of individual liberty that has been proposed since the cruel period of [the Republican's] *Reconstruction.*

In those days when the Southland lay prostrate, crushed, harshly ruled by military governors [appointed by the Republican], *the Congress, in which the South was misrepresented in many cases by residents of Northern States, rammed through the* [Republican's] ***notorious Civil Rights Act of 1875. This was one of the infamous 'force bill' designed to tear apart the very fabric of southern life.***

Fortunately for the Nation, those aggrieved had recourse to the Constitution. Even though amended under questionable circumstances, the Constitution was our salvation because when [the Democrats challenged the issue in court] *and the Supreme Court put the Civil Rights of 1875 to the ultimate test, it was found wanting.*

Mr. President, I for one, am going to devote my best efforts to returning this resurrected [Republican] *statute to its grave."*

Everett Dirksen Republican from Illinois addressed the Senate with the following: *"...To my fellow Senators to consider this issue in the light of national interest. It is a phase that came close to the late President Kennedy. It is a phase that comes close to our former majority leader, who now occupies his exalted position. I want to do what I think is in the interest of the present and future wellbeing of probably the only real, true free republic that still remains on God's footstool. I shall cooperate. I shall do my best. When the times come, when the deliberations are at the end, and all facets of the matter have been carefully considered and discussed, I shall be prepared to render judgment, and I shall have no apology to make to any group anywhere, for the course that I shall ultimately pursue."*

Emanuel Celler, Democrat from New York said. *"Mr. Chairman, this is an opportunity for which we have been anxiously awaiting. You know,* **the Lord's best gifts to us are not things, but opportunities,** *and we now have the bestowed upon us a golden opportunity to do a great thing.*

Both parties joined hands. We felt we represented a cause. We shunned a political issue. I am grateful to the ranking member of the Republican Party on the Judiciary Committee, the gentleman form Ohio [Mr. McCulloch]. He and I labored incessantly fashioning the bill. I pay tribute to him and his fellow Republicans who stood by him.... **The demonstration and violence of the recent months have served to point up what many of us have known for years: That this nation can no longer abide the moral outrage of discrimination."**

William McCullough, Republican form Ohio followed with these comments: *"No Statutory law can completely end discrimination under attack by this legislation. Intelligent work and vigilance by members of all races will be required, for many years, before discrimination completely disappears. To create hope of immediate and complete success can only promote conflict and result brooding and despair....*

No force or fear, then, but belief in the inherent equality of man induces me to support this legislation.

I believe in the right of each individual to have his constitutional rights guaranteed. On the other hand, he must always be prepared to shoulder the obligations and assume the burdens of citizenship.

No one would suggest that the Negro receives equality of treatment and equality of opportunity in many fields of activity, today. Well-formed persons, everywhere, admit that in all sections of the country – North, South, East, and West – the Negro continues to face the barriers of racial intolerance and discrimination. Hundreds of thousands of citizens are denied the basic right to vote. Thousands of school districts remain segregated. Decent hotel and eating accommodations frequently lie hundreds of miles apart for the Negro traveler. Parks, playgrounds, and golf courses continue to be off limits to Negroes whose tax money go to support them. Many programs continue to be operated in a discriminatory manner. These, and many more such conditions point the way toward the need for additional legislation.

I recommend H.R. 7152, as amended, to all my colleagues from wheresoever they come."

1965 Voting Rights Act

The 1965 Voting Rights Act began with a speech from President Lyndon B. Johnson to the Congress of the United States on March 15, 1965. The followings are a few excerpts from that speech:

" Mr. Speaker, Mr. President, Members of the Congress, I speak tonight for the dignity of man and the destiny of democracy. ...In our time we have come to live with moments of great crisis. Our lives have been marked with debate about great issues; issues of war and peace, of prosperity and depression. But rarely in any time does an issue lay bare the secret heart of America itself.... The issue of equal rights for American Negroes is such an issue. And should we defeat every enemy, should we double our wealthy and conquer the stars, and still be unequal to this issue, then we will have failed as a people and as a nation.

*For with a country as with a person, **"What is a man profited, if he shall gain the whole world and lose his own soul."***

...To deny a man his hopes because of his color or race, his religion or place of birth – is not only to do injustice, it is to deny America and to dishonor the dead who gave their lives for American freedom ...Yet the harsh fact is that in many places in this country men and women are kept from voting because they are Negroes ... All Americans must have the right to vote. And we are going to give that right.

*...Above the pyramid on the great seal of the United States its says – in Latin – **God has favored our undertaking." God will not favor everything we do. It is rather our duty to divine His will. But I cannot help believing that He truly understands and that he really favors the undertaking that we begin here tonight."***

The Purpose: With bipartisan support, the debates started on April 22, 1965 to eliminate the voting irregularities in the Democratically controlled south by providing congressional enforcement of the 15th Amendment in the election process.

Democrat's Opposition: Several participated in the debate, but the primary persons who engaged in the debates, were Republican Senators, Everett Dirksen of Illinois and Jacob Javits from New York Democratic and Senators Sam Ervin of North Carolina, and Herman Talmadge from Georgia.

Sam Erivin, *"This bill contains a provision which condemns without judicial trial the States of Alabama, Mississippi, Louisiana,*

Georgia, South Carolina and Virginia and 34 counties in North Carolina; does it not?"

Senator Dirksen: *"Yes; I do not believe it condemns the States. It takes account of a condition that has existed in those States. We are seeking to remedy a condition that exists with respect to citizens of the United States. We go to the heart of the problem and seek to supply a remedy that we think is constitutional and non-punitive."*

Herman Talmadge Democrat from Georgia: *"We were told last year that with the passage of a broad, all-encompassing civil rights bill, which covered almost everything that the mind of man could conceive, that there would not be any further need of a civil rights bill. Would not the bill deny to the States of Louisiana, Alabama, Mississippi, Georgia, North Carolina, and certain carefully selected counties in other areas the right to apply any literacy standards whatsoever for their voters?"*

Regarding literacy test, **Jacob Javits respond**: *"Think of the situation, for example in Mississippi, where whites are asked to interpret the following provision of the State Constitution: The Senate shall consist of Members chosen every 4 years by the qualified electors of the several districts. "Negroes are asked to interpret sections of the Constitution dealing with tax exemptions, the judicial sale of land, eminent domain, concurrent jurisdiction of chancery and circuit courts and habeas corpus. [And] What about deprivation going back for a century, which inhered in segregated schools resulting in a median education level of the sixth grade for Negroes in Mississippi, as compared with an 11th grade median for whites? Then there is the intimidation by public officials; there are the bombings and shooting, the burnings, the beatings; and quite apart from them, the denial of surplus food to Negroes who persist in their attempt to register, as in Humphreys County, Miss.; or the boycotting of Negroes who had the temerity to register by cutting off their bank loans and their grocery store credit."* The debates started on April 22, 1965

1968 Civil Rights Acts

The Purpose: The bi-partisan bill was designed to protect Negroes and civil-rights workers by outlawing racially-motivated acts of violence against persons exercising Fourteen Amendment rights. It also had a fair housing component to ban discrimination in housing.

Democrats Opposition: The Democrats opposing the bill included Lawrence Fountain and Sam Ervin, Democrats from North Carolina. **Fountain said,** *"If this bill becomes law, it will be a clear invitation to this tiny band of agitators to continue to foment strife and fuel civil disorder. We have seen too much of that lately and why we seem to want to nourish it is beyond me. But that is exactly what the impact of this bill would be."*

Sam Ervin said, *" It would be easy to defeat their efforts if they were evil-minded men professing bad ends. Unfortunately for the cause of sound constitutional government, however, they are men of good intentional, who are willing to do constitutional evil because they believe good will result from it. In so doing, they emulate the example of Mother Eve, who succumbed to the temptation to eat the forbidden fruit because she saw "it was pleasant to the eyes," and believed it to be "good for food," and was satisfied that it "would make one wise."*

"The men who seek to destroy or impair these constitutional principles and constitutional rights, claim that it is necessary for the Federal Government **to deprive all Americans of basic economic, legal personal and property rights to give equality to 20 million Negro Americans."**

John Stennis, the Democrat from Mississippi said, *" I wish to be clear that I oppose this measure in most of its major particulars, and that I have been one of many who have worked to avoid it. I believe particularly with reference to the passage of the open housing legislation, that it will prove to be a grave mistake and one of the gravest that the Senate has ever made."*

1972 Equal Employment Act

The Purpose: To assure and promote equal opportunity in Employment.

The voting record on this piece of legislation shows that there were Democrats who also opposed this bill. Democrats: 155 voted for and 79 voted against. Republicans: 130 voted for and 26 voted against. This bill was passed during the Nixon Administration. Shortly after the passage of this bill, Nixon issued Executive Order 11478 which paved the way for Affirmative Action programs, a program that included quotas, goals and timetables.

79 Democrats Voted Against
1972 Equal Employment Opportunity Act

Abernethy, Abourezk, Andrews (Ala), Aspinall, Baring, Begich, Dveill, Brinkley, Burleson (Texas), Cabell, Caffery, Chappell, Chisholm, Clay, Colmer, Conyers, Daniel, Danmiel (VA), Davis (GA), Davis (S.C.), Dellums, Denholm, Dent, Diggs, Dorn, Dowdy, Drinan, Edmondson, Fisher, Flowers, Dlynt, Ford (W.D. Mich.), Gettys, Giaimo, Grasso, Green, (ore.), Griffin, Griffith, Hagan, Haley, Hebert, Henderson, Hull, Hungate, Jones (Ala.), Jones (Tenn), Kazen, Kee, Landrum, Lennon, McMillan, Mahon, Mathis, Mills (W.D. Ark.), Mink, Nedzi, Nichols, O'Hara, Passman, Patman, Poage, Purcell, Randall, Rarick, Roberts, Runnels, Satterfield, Shipley, Sikes, Slack, Staggers, Steed, Stephens, Stubblefield, Stuckey, Teague (Texas), Waggonner, Watts, Whitten, Young (Texas).

21 Democrats Did Not Vote

Abbitt, Albert, Alexander, Anderson (Tenn), Clark, Edwards, (La.), Evans, (Colo.) Hansen (Wash), Hathaway, Jarman, Karth,

Long (La.), McCormack, Mollohan, Montgomery, Murphy (Ill.), Pryor (Ark), Roybal, Sullivan, Symington, Udall.

After reviewing the evidence, many believe America would have never experience racism to the degree that it has, had not the Democrats meticulously and intentionally promoted it through

- Racist Legislation
- Terrorist Organizations
- Negative Communications
- Bias Education
- Relentless Intimidation
- And Flawed adjudication.

The racism established by and promoted by members of the Democratic Party, *affected* and *infected* the entire nation from 1863 to 2003. The records will show that the Democratic Party has never issued a formal apology for their past racist agenda and activities. Such activities have had a profound negative impact on an entire race of people, both economically and psychologically, for several decades. There is a clear case for reparations based on the atrocities committed by the members of the Democratic Party from 1863-2003.

Source of Appendix H

Statutory History of United States
　　Editor, Professor Bernard Schwartz of New York University
　　School of Law

Commerce Clearing House: Voting Records on House Bills
　　Prentice Hall's American Nation

The Thirteenth Amendment

Fernando Wood's Comments	Pages 44+46	Statutory History
James Wilson's Comments	Page 29+35	Statutory History

1866 Civil Rights Acts

Willard Saulsbury's Comments	Page 113	Statutory History
Reverdy Johnson's Comments	Page 119	Statutory History
William Fessenden's Comments	Page 119	Statutory History
Martin Thayer's Comments	Pages 130-131	Statutory History
Michael Kerr's Comments	Pages 135-136	Statutory History

The First Reconstruction Act of 1867

Ben Tillman's Comments	Page 427	American Nation

The Fourteenth Amendment

Andrew Rogers' Comments	Page 246	Statutory History

The Fifteenth Amendment

The Enforcement Act of 1870

The Force Act of 1871

Ku Klux Klan Act of 1871

Civil Rights act of 1875

Repeal Act of 1894

The Silent Years 1875-1957

1957 Civil Rights Act

1960 Civil Rights Act

1964 Civil Rights Act

Thomas Abernethy's Comments   Page 1128   Statutory History
Donald Matthews's Comments   Page 1135   Statutory History
Sam Ervin's Comments   Page 1307   Statutory History
Robert Byrd's Comments   Page 1341   Statutory History
Olin Johnston's Comments   Page 1404   Statutory History
Howard Smith's Comments   Page 1421   Statutory History
William McCullough Comments   Page 1112   Statutory History
Everett Dirksen Comments   Page 1141   Statutory History
John Sparkman's Comments   Pages 1151-53   Statutory History

1965 Voting Rights Act

President Johnson's Address   Page 1506   Statutory History
Sam Ervin's Comments   Page 1512   Statutory History
Everett Dirksen's Comments   Page 1512   Statutory History
Herman Talmadge's Comments   Page 1542   Statutory History
Jacob Javit's Comments   Page 1575   Statutory History

1968 Civil Rights Act

Lawrence Fountain'c Comments   Page 1668   Statutory History
Everett Dirksen   Page 1684   Statutory History
Sam Ervin's Comments   Page 1686   Statutory History
John Stennis' Comments   Page 1757   Statutory History

1972 Equal Employment Opportunity Act

Republican and Democrats' Voting Records From Commerce Clearing
House.

Other Sources

Rise & Fall of Jim Crow a PBS four part series (2002) produced by
Quest Productions, Videoline Productions and Thirteen/WNET

Appendix I

Similarities Between

The Nazi Party & The Democratic Party

A person once asked: *"If a Jew would never join the Nazi Party, why would a black join the Democratic Party given the fact that Democrats committed similar acts against the blacks that the Nazi's committed against the Jews?"*

The following is a comparison between what happened to Jews under Germany's Nazi Party vs what happened to Blacks under the South's Democratic Party. This comparison is in no way an attempt to minimize the tremendous mass murder of the Jews during the holocaust.

The tragedy and the horrors that they experienced cannot be compared to any other human tragedy in modern history. This analysis is only to show that up to the time of the mass murders (of the Jews 1933-1945) there were striking similarities between what happened to Blacks under Democratic rule and what happened to the Jews under Nazi rule.

Oppression

From 1933 to 1945 members of the Nazi Party oppressed millions of the Jews (12 years). From 1854 to 1960, members of the Democratic Party oppressed millions of blacks (106 years).

Racist Legislation

The Nazi Party passed racist legislation to deny Jews their rights as citizens. The Democratic Party passed racist legislation to deny blacks their rights as citizens, including, Black Codes, Jim Crow Laws and a multitude of other repressive legislation at the state level. Congressional records also show that various members of the Democratic Party voted against every piece of key Civil

Rights Legislation through 1988, while various members of the Republican Party voted for them.

Education
The Nazi Party refused to let Jewish children attend public schools with German children. The Democratic Party refused to let Blacks attend school with white children.

Forced Labor
The Nazi Party forced the Jews to work in labor camps giving them nothing or little in return. During slavery and under the Black Codes members of the Democratic Party forced blacks to work on plantations giving them little to nothing in return.

Captivity
Under Nazi rule, Jews were force to do hard labor in Concentration Camps. After Reconstruction, under Democratic rule (in the South) thousands of blacks were sentenced to work in inhumane prison labor camps building railroads,draining swamps and working in mines. Several private corporations were the benefactors of this free labor.

Denied Citizenship
Under Nazi rule, the party took away the Jew's citizenship. Under Democratic rule the Democrats exhausted every effort to deny blacks their rights as citizen starting with the Dred Scott decision and followed by collectively voting against the 13th 14th and 15th amendment and consequently, passing Black Codes and Jim Crow Laws.

Forbidding Intermarriage
Under Nazi rule Jews were prohibited from marrying Germans. Under the Democratic rule (using Black Codes and other legislation) blacks were prohibited from marrying whites (see opposition to 1866 Civil Rights Act).

Businesses Taken & Destroyed

The Nazi Party confiscated and/or destroyed Jewish businesses. Southern Democrats also confiscated land and destroyed black businesses (1867-1945). According to Associated Press (in 2002), under Democratic control, southern blacks lost several million acres of Land. Wilmington, North Carolina; Tulsa, Oklahoma; and Rosewood, Florida were just three of the many predominately black southern towns and communities that were destroyed.

Synagogues and Churches Destroyed

Under Nazi rule, synagogues were destroyed. Under Democratic rule, several black churches were burned and bomb during a 150-year period.

Forced To Live In Ghettos

The Nazi Party forced the Jews into ghettos. Members of the Democratic Party denied blacks the right to live where they chose, thus blacks like the Jews, were forced to live in their own ghettos.

Terrorist Activities & Murder

The Nazi Party used their SS division to terrorize and murder Jews at random. During a 150 year period, members of the Democratic Party and their various terrorist organizations (including the Klan) terrorized and murdered blacks at random (see chapter four and chapter seven).

Hatred

The Nazi Party promoted hatred against Jews and Blacks. The Democratic Party and their terrorist organizations also promoted hatred against Blacks (and later on, Jews, Catholics, and homosexuals).

Political Offices

Under Nazi rule Jews were prohibited from running for public office. Under Democratic rule, blacks were beaten, killed, and driven out of office to discourage them from seeking public office. Democrats also printed cards similar to baseball cards to identify black officer holders for the sole purpose of targeting them for terrorist attacks and intimidation.

Destruction of Lives

The Nazi Party, through their legislative efforts and terrorist activities took the lives of millions of Jews in a 12-year period. Under Democratic rule through their terrorist activities and legislative practices they took the lives and affected the lives of millions of African Americans (including slavery). The *entire* black race was terrorized over a span of 150 years.

Torture

The Nazi Party through their SS division tortured millions of Jews. The Democratic Party through their various terrorist organizations hung, shot, mutilated, and burned to death, countless numbers of blacks during a 150-year period. African American History Professor, John Hope Franklin said the atrocities committed against blacks are *"too numerous to list and that they would defy our imagination."*

Apology

Eventually the Jews did receive an apology. However the records will show that the Democratic Party has never issued an apology for the atrocities that they committed against blacks in the name of their Party, or for the in-humane acts committed by members of their terrorist organizations.

Fact-Finding Investigative Sources

The Abolitionist Legacy From Reconstruction to the NAACP
Professor James McPherson of Princeton University

The Struggle for Equality
Professor James McPherson of Princeton University

Charles Sumner
Professor David Herbert Donald of Harvard University

Disuniting of America
Former Associate Professor Arthur M. Schlesinger Jr. of Harvard University

The Abolitionist Sisterhood
Professor Jean Fagan Yellin of Pace University

Black Americans
John Hope Franklin

Why We Can't Wait
Rev. Dr. Martin Luther King

The Causes of the Civil War
Professor Kenneth M. Stampp of University of California At Berkeley

The Myth of Separation
David Barton

God's Politician
Garth Lean

From Slavery To Freedom
John Hope Franklin and Alfred A. Moss

The Fabulous Democrats
David L. Cohn

The Republicans: A History of Their Party
Professor Malcolm Moos of Johns Hopkins University

The Negro Almanac: A Reference Work on African Americans
Harry Ploski and James Williams

Black Women in America: An Historical Encyclopedia
Darlene Clark Hine

A Hand Up: Black Philanthropy and Self-Help In America
Emmett D. Carson

Economic Empowerment Through the Church
Gregory Reed

When the Game Was Black and White
Bruce Chadwick

Raising Black Children
Professor Alvin F. Poussaint and James P. Comer

Black Families in Therapy: A Multisystem Approach
Professor Nancy Boyd-Franklin

Conspiracy to Destroy Black Boys
Jawanza Kunjufu

The Negro Family in the United States
Frazier E. Franklin

Black Lies, White Lies
Tony Brown

The Way of the Bootstrapper
Floyd Flake

Playing America's Game
Michael L. Cooper

A History of Black America
Professor Howard O. Lindsey of DePaul University

Reconstruction After the Civil War
Professor John Hope Franklin

Reconstruction: The Great Experiment
Professor Allen W. Trelease

The Clash of the Cultures
Joseph A. Raelin

Counseling the Culturally Different
Professor David Sue

To Raise a Jewish Child
Rabbi Halevy Donin

Bar Mitzvah
Sara Silberstein Swartz

A Documentary History of the Negro People in the United States
Herbert Aptheker (Foreword by W.E.B. DuBois)

Black Business in the New South
Walter B. Weare

Booker T. Washington
Jan Gleiter and Kathleen Thompson

George Washington Carver: An American Biography
Rackham Holt

The American Presidents
Grolier Books

A Documentary History of The Negro People In The United States
Herbert Aptheker (Foreword by W.E.B. DuBois)

America's God and Country Encyclopedia of Quotations
William J. Federer

The Holy Bible (King James and NIV)

News Media Sources

Playboy Magazine Interview With Dr. Martin Luther King

Washington Post November 1, 1993 issue

Time Magazine September 23, 1991 issue

The Seattle Times December 14, 1993 issue

The Seattle Times December 2, 2001 issue

USA Today February 24, 1992 issue

Christianity Today March 1996 issue

Christianity Today June 11, 2001 issue

Ebony Magazine November 2000 issue

Ebony Magazine January 1993 issue

Newsweek Magazine June 1, 1998 issue

Savoy Magazine May 2001 issue

The Economist Magazine August 18, 2001 issue

The New York Times August 22, 2001 issue

Exclusive interview with Buck O'Neil, founder of the Negro Baseball Museum

Trial transcripts of Charles Fairchild vs. Secretary Labor Robert Riech

Statistics From

Black Americans: A Statistical Sourcebook
Center of Disease Control
NFTA Conference
U.S. Department of Commerce Statistical Abstract
Christianity Today March 1996

Index

Index

D

Davis, Ossie, 84
death rates among young blacks, 73–74
Democratic Leadership Council, 79
Democratic Party
    and black voters, 43, 45–46, 81
    call for cooperation with the Republicans, 112
    contrasted with the Republican Party, 47–49, 52–53, 106–110, 121
    courting the black vote, 67, 102–103
    installation of Governor Kellogg, 63, 101
    intimidation at the polls, 56–58
    lack of efficacy, 71–72
    origins of the Ku Klux Klan, 99
    racist policies summarized, 99–110, 112
    terrorist acts, 64, 101–102, 117
Depression of 1929, 45–46
desegregation, 25–30, 35
discrimination in employment, 23–24, 88–90
Disuniting of America (Schlesinger), 27
Documentary History of Negro People (Aptheker), 63–64
Doin, Halvey (Rabbi), 28
Domefree, Isabella (Sojourner Truth), 8
Donald, David Hebert, 101
Douglas, Stephen, 53
Douglass, Frederick, 9–10, 134–135, *136*
drug offenses, pardons, 79
Duke University Divinity School, 30
Dunant, Jean Henri, 122

E

Ebony Magazine, 77–79
Economic Empowerment Through the Church (Reed), 133–134
Economist, 85
education through faith-based organizations, 116–121
educational challenges, 19–20
Eichhorn, Dennis P., 11–12
Eisenhower, 52–53
Emancipation Proclamation, 52, 55–56
Emperor's New Clothes, 71–72
employment opportunity, 21, 23–24
Equal Employment Opportunity Commission, 23, 76, 109–110

F

The Fabulous Democrats (Cohn), 103–104
Fairchild v. Reich, 89
faith as a stepping stone, 125–126, 132
faith-based programs, 113–123
family structure, changes since King's death, 20
farmland, black ownership, 103
federal employment, firings, 74
Ferguson v. Plessy, 65
Fisk University, 119–120
Flake, Floyd, 40, 94, *95*
Flanagan, Edward J. (Father), 122
Franklin, John Hope, views on
    Democratic Party as a source of violence, 56
    election of 1933, 45
    prevailing Democratic views, 67
    role of black clergy, 12–13
    From Slavery to Freedom, 100–101
    white supremacy in politics, 65
Franklin, Nancy Boyd, 2, 14
Freedmen's Bureau, 99
freedom, buying, 16
Freeman, Richard, 37–38
From Slavery to Freedom (Franklin), 100–101
Fugitive Slave Laws, 114

G

Getting ready to die young, 73–74
Gibbons, Hannah, 115
God-given mission, 143–144
Godly principles for directing action, 112, 132–133
Gore, Al, 77–79
government funding for self-help programs, 127–128
Grant, President, 63, 101
Great Depression, 45–46
Greeley, Horace, 55

H

Hampton Normal Agricultural Institute, 5
A Hand Up (Carson), 134
Harper's Ferry, raid on arsenal, 114
hate groups
    See specific hate groups